f

Fusion Press
20 Queen Anne Street
London W1M 0AY
UK
email: sheenadewan@compuserve.com
website: http://www.visionpaperbacks.demon.co.uk

Originally published in Australia by Allen & Unwin

Design: Nickolai Globe
Layout: Justine Hounam
Printed and bound in Great Britain by Biddles Ltd.

ISBN: 1-901250-67-9

Self-Sexual Healing

Finding Pleasure Within

Jo-Anne Baker

Contents

Contents

I dedicate this book to my parents, who have been a constant source of love and support in my life.

Acknowledgements

I would like to thank all those who have inspired me and given me their words of wisdom. To Kimberly O'Sullivan, for her invaluable help in developing the manuscript – I wouldn't have been able to write the book without you. To Esme Homes, for her love and support. To Ruth Ostrow, a wonderful friend and inspiration. To C. Moore Hardy, for her wonderful photography in our workshops. To Elizabeth Burton, for her great striptease classes. To Belinda Abel, a constant source of friendship. To my agent David Holland, for his guidance. To Rosie King, for the help she has always given me.

JO-ANNE BAKER
JUNE 1998

Foreword

Do we really need another book about sex?

The answer is a resounding "Yes!". Certainly there's limited room for another how-to sex manual that promises sexual ecstasy by simply pushing all the right buttons. However, men and women of all ages will definitely benefit from a book like Jo-Anne Baker's which encourages us to explore and express our own unique version of sexuality.

No two people are alike in their sexual responses, needs, awareness and expectations. The true beauty of our sexuality is that it is profoundly idiosyncratic and personal, a deep reflection of our singularity and human perfection. In recognition of this, Jo-Anne's approach is a personalised one, giving readers plenty of opportunities, through exercises, to workshop their sexuality in a safe and non-confronting way. Using an eclectic mix of techniques from both the East and the West, meshing the alternative and the traditional, readers are led along a gentle path, a path that can eventually lead them to a sexuality transformed by healing.

Jo-Anne presents sex in a holistic context of self-awareness and self-loving, self-acceptance and self-actualisation. Sex is essentially an inner experience that we can choose to share with another if we wish, or not. Jo-Anne clearly makes the point that there is much more to sex that genital-to-genital activity. Sex is an emotional, physical, sensual, intellectual and spiritual experience through which we can learn more about ourselves and our partners. Instead of giving "sexual recipes", Jo-Anne focuses our attention inwards – to our own thoughts, feelings and desires, the sources of our erotic needs. She shows us ways of truly expressing and fulfilling these needs. Jo-Anne's premise is that you alone hold the key to your sexual satisfaction and her strategies can help you to turn that key and free yourself from sexual shame and unhappiness.

For decades so-called experts have been telling people how to run their sex lives – how to think, how to feel, how to respond. Sexism has been rife – men act like this and women like that. Widespread ageism dictates that sex is only for young, perfect bodies, and anyone over fifty need not apply. The result has been a narrow and restrictive idea about how sex should be, perpetuated and disseminated by sexually explicit books, movies, erotica and pornography. The causes of sexual dissatisfaction are obvious. People know very little about sex and much of what they know is wrong. This ignorance, coupled with totally unrealistic expectations, leads to performance anxiety and loss of sexual enjoyment. Sex has sadly become an Olympic sport with everyone going for gold on all occasions.

There is a wise saying, "Don't cut the man to fit the coat. Cut the coat to fit the man." Instead of men and women lopping off parts of their sexuality to fit in with an unrealistic stereotype of sexual functioning, doesn't it make better sense to expand our narrow social construct of sex to allow for the widely varied erotic functioning of individuals? Jo-Anne presents us with practical ways to broaden our thinking about sex and overcome long-held emotional blocks.

A happy, healthy sexuality is an integrated expression of our past, our present and our dreams for the future. Jo-Anne gives insight into the true spirit of nourishing sexuality. This is the heart and soul of our sexuality, a healing resource available to all of us if we can learn to tap into it. This book will help to show you how.

DR ROSIE KING
JUNE 1998

Introduction

This book will give you the ability to become the sexually fulfilled, happy person you deserve to be, regardless of your age, gender, sexual orientation or relationship status. It will help you to make the changes you want in your life and show you that feeling sensual and alive depends on yourself, not anyone else. If you are single, do not wait for a lover to come into your life to begin to sexually grow and heal. The most effective healing you can do is by yourself, first by relaxing and learning to trust yourself and your body's sensations, and then by taking this expansion into everyday life. If you are in a relationship, remember that it is important to make time for your own sexual growth, as it is hard to nurture a relationship with another if you do not come from a secure place in yourself.

Sexuality is an area of lifelong fun and adventure which does not start and finish just with your genitals. I have now been running workshops on sexuality and doing private sessions with individual clients and couples for over ten years. This has given me a rare insight into human sexual problems, and I have seen many people, irrespective of their background, raise similar emotional issues. These are a lack of self-love and acceptance, an inability to trust, poor communication and being stuck in past pain.

Everyone's sexual journey is unique, there is no one right way to fix up your sex life. Healing can come in many different forms and frequently in ways you do not expect.

It is important that each person explore different approaches to healing because our backgrounds and life experiences are so diverse that not one style of therapy will work for everyone. When you work with this book you will undoubtedly find you respond more strongly to some chapters than others. While each person's journey looks totally different, when I am in a room full of people in a group session, discussing our issues, I experience an interlinking of all our lives.

The exercises and tips I have put together will give you a way to explore your own unique healing process and tap into your creativity, and they can give you lots of pleasure and fun. The case histories are from people I have met through my work, and their stories will give you a new insight into how people have integrated the exercises and techniques into their lives. My approach to successful healing is to start from a position of commitment to your own growth, without imposing a fixed, desired outcome. I am not a doctor or a psychologist; the work I do has come from dealing with my own sexual repression and reaching a state of inner peace and acceptance. I have done a great deal of training over many years, and in many different disciplines, and draw on all of this in my work.

How to use this book

In the 1930s and '40s, sexologist Wilhelm Reich identified four stages of the orgasm cycle: tension, charge, release and relaxation. I have based much of my work on his theory and this is reflected in the exercises in this book, particularly in Chapter 2 and the erotic massage in Chapter 5. Surprising as it may sound, it is crucial to change your breathing patterns in order to heal. Our breath is our life force and is essential to a happy, healthy sex life. The techniques in Chapter 2 will show you how to use breath and movement to pulse sexual energy throughout your body. All the exercises in this book are designed to take you deeper into yourself, so it is important to put aside time to practise the exercises. Some require a regular commitment while others might need to be done only a couple of times. Once you are comfortable with the specific structure of an exercise you can expand and become creative and add extra elements. If exercises are part of a sequence, it is important that you do the entire set. Some people will experience a shift after doing the exercises only once, but if it takes you a longer period of time that is all right. Persist in doing them and the change will come.

Integrate what you have been going through after doing these exercises for a period of weeks, or months, and if you need to take time out, do so. I encourage you to keep a journal of your experiences during these exercises to help you pace your growth and understanding.

Most of the exercises are designed to be done without a partner. For the few, excluding Chapter 5, which need to be done with a partner ask a trusted friend, close sibling or your lover to accompany you. Healing takes different forms, and the support of a good therapist as you start to explore and grow can be very beneficial. Interactive or transpersonal psychotherapy, such as Gestalt, psychodrama, Eye Movement Desensitisation Reprocessing (EMDR), transactional analysis, and deep-body work can be supportive and beneficial.

Searching for sexual wholeness

Sex is a natural part of life, on the most basic level we all come out of sex and we need to embrace it and allow it to be a source of self-nurturance and love.

The work I do is disguised under the label of sexuality, but it is actually about bringing the feminine, intuitive side back into our lifelong pursuit of pleasure and sensuality, both personally and in relations with others. While the 1960s sexual revolution freed up ideas about sex, in many ways the deep connection between love and sex was lost. There is another revolution going on at the moment in which people are searching for a deeper connection between their personal happiness and their sexual fulfilment. People no longer want to feel the pain of emotional disconnectedness.

While sexual abuse and trauma are now widely acknowledged as deeply scarring, there are also other issues people have to heal: a difficulty in feeling at ease in the body (anorexia and bulimia are becoming increasingly common amongst all age groups and socioeconomic backgrounds); an inability to have the relationship you want (two out of three committed relationships end); unresolved sexual problems, manifesting in women having difficulty with orgasm, men with impotency, and both sexes having great problems creating intimacy in their emotional and sexual lives. It does not matter if you are with someone for five minutes, one day, or an entire lifetime, you will not be sexually fulfilled unless you have first developed a love of yourself, which you can then take into your relating.

My journey, like everyone else's, has been about pursuit of happiness, I and the work I do comes from this place. From a very early age I had questioned the meaning of life. My father was a veterinarian and we lived adjacent to his surgery, so as a young child I spent many hours in his consulting rooms with sick animals. I was in a realm without words, where touch and sensation became a means to understanding life, as the dogs and cats could only convey their pain, or contentment, with their eyes. This early experience taught me the importance of listening to the body's wisdom, going within and trusting my body's sensations to tell me what I needed to do to heal. In turn this has enabled me to experience great depths of pleasure.

In my teens I explored yoga and meditation and noticed how relaxed I felt, but wanting to experience more bodily connection and a greater sense of aliveness I did dance classes and swam competitively. My first real sexual exploration happened when I was eighteen and listening to George Harrison sing "My Sweet Lord". As I sat cross-legged on the floor, fully clothed, I started rocking backward and forward in time with the beat. Breathing deeply, I became more and more absorbed in the sounds, and suddenly to my surprise I felt an amazing rush of energy coming from my genitals and pulsing throughout my entire body. I had no idea what had happened and I had to wait many more years to understand these sensations and to again experience such a depth of pleasure.

As the years passed I looked for a different understanding of life, one which was beyond the traditional Western model. Eastern philosophy became the key to my search and in my early twenties I travelled throughout Asia, South America and the USA, eventually living and studying in the USA and London. These wonderful travel experiences made me realise I had a choice about how I wanted to look at life and the people around me. I chose to look for people and places to help me grow and expand.

In one of my old travel diaries I wrote: "I see the negative qualities when I look at someone, but I also see the beauty, and once I have seen that it means so much more. To see in this way is to experience a new type of warmth and happiness, which brings a depth of love and wonder." Looking back on this now, I see I have used this insight as a way of working with the people I have counselled. I focus on each person's innate inner beauty and work from that point. I teach my clients to connect to this place because this is the key to their healing.

I had a passion to heal people, initially attracted to Western herbalism, which I studied briefly, and then traditional Japanese diet. I had an idealistic approach, where I could see traditional Western medicine working with Eastern or alternative techniques. I studied, and eventually taught, vegetarian and cordon bleu cooking in Australia and London, and this led to an interest in macrobiotics, which I studied in Australia and Boston. During a brief stint in the whole-foods industry I introduced food free of sugar and preservatives to schools and hospitals.

While diet can be an amazing adjunct to physiological and emotional healing, I realised there were many emotional factors in life that could not be explained by what we eat and drink, so I went on a deeper search. I studied astrology in Boston and in Australia and still find the discipline of astrology invaluable in my life. Close friends ask for planetary advice to this day.

A major transformation happened in my life when I was in my mid-twenties and became a follower of Rajneesh, who was often described as the sex guru. Rajneesh emphasised experiencing things totally, with body-oriented meditation and breath becoming a focus to connect with the vital energy of life. I also explored many alternate therapies: rebirthing, bioenergetics, past-life regression, hypnotherapy, body work, encounter and Gestalt therapy. These practices gave me a great understanding of the integration of the mind and body as I learned to experience deep levels of pleasure, bliss and meditation. During this time the exploration of sexuality's essence became of prime importance in my life. Experimentation and living out my repressed sexuality led me to play in a new realm, but it took me another ten years to learn the depths of sexual pleasure that are possible.

When the movie *Sacred Sex* was released in Australia in 1991 I started to promote workshops which had been organised to coincide with its release. Through this I met Annie Sprinkle, the American sex educator and performance artist, who became a dear friend and a catalyst to the development of the work I do now: helping people find more pleasure in their life. Women who had done the workshops I organised asked my advice on which books, videos and sex toys to buy to improve their sex life. I started researching products and quickly realised that no-one was catering to women's needs or answering their intimate questions.

In 1992 I went to San Francisco and while there did a course on sexuality. As fate would have it, also doing the course was Dell Williams, who in 1974 had set up the first women's sex shop in the world, Eve's Garden in New York City. This business was unique because it was the first sex shop to be set up for women and by women. All previous sex shops had been run by men, with their products for women designed by men based on what they imagined a woman wanted. This was usually far from the truth.

Talking to Dell I quickly realised how important such a shop would be in Australia. I envisioned a sensual but safe environment where women could have their most intimate questions answered, buy high quality products, and do courses on increasing their sexual knowledge and pleasure. In San Francisco's women's sex shop Good Vibrations, I bought my first vibrator and dildo. I was in my late thirties and already very sexually aware, but my new-found toys gave me a different area of sexual exploration and another dimension of sexual fun. But why were these products not available in Australia? When I arrived back home I already had a plan in mind.

When they saw the importance of what I wanted to create my parents became involved, supporting me emotionally and financially, and The Pleasure Spot came into being as a mail-order business which sold quality sexual products to women with complete confidentiality. My catalogue contained vibrators, dildos, videos, soft whips, feathers, lubricants and books. I started to manufacture my own silicon dildos, in beautiful colours, shaped like whales, dolphins and even goddesses, so that women could have the opportunity to buy non-phallic ones. This was the first time such products had been made and sold in Australia.

Eighteen months later, with business booming, I went overseas to research the feasibility of opening my own shop. I visited all the women's sex shops I could find in the US, London and Amsterdam, sourced products, and talked to female sex experts about what they recommended. Highly enthusiastic, I returned to Australia and expanded The Pleasure Spot from my home to a full-time retail shop, which has gone from strength to strength. Thousands and thousands of people from all over Australia have contacted me to buy products, do courses and individual counselling sessions.

For many of these people this was the first time they had explored their sexual pleasure, or sought to sexually grow and develop. The Pleasure Spot has gained recognition and support from doctors, therapists, sexual health clinics, and most importantly by word of mouth from satisfied customers. I have done numerous radio, magazine and television interviews, and also run a sex information line. I have experienced great joy in my work, helping individual women have more pleasure in their life and couples have more intimacy and connection. I am privileged to get wonderful feedback from women, the most common being "I have never spoken to anyone about this issue," or, "Now I know I am not the only one who feels this way."

Even though I set out to establish a business for women, men have also been enthusiastic clients of The Pleasure Spot. Many men visit seeking advice on what to buy their female partners, wanting to know how to improve their love life, or to attend the courses I run.

As my customers started asking for more personal advice and help I saw them privately, and then started to get referrals from therapists and doctors whose clients were struggling with long-term sexual issues. I worked with these clients using body-oriented therapy, and had good results and positive feedback. My private counselling has grown from this basis. The therapists who refer people to me often comment that I seem relaxed and accepting of my own sexuality, so they feel confident in sending their patients to me. I can empathise with any sexual issue because I have struggled with so many of my own.

As my individual counselling work developed, I intuitively drew on my past experiences and broke down my own sexual fears and barriers. I came from a sexually repressed background and I clearly remember an early boyfriend telling me how sexually inhibited I appeared. So I have had to do a lot of personal work to feel at ease in my body. The basis of my work is that sexual and emotional trauma are located not only in our memories but in our bodies and this can be seen in the way we move and hold ourselves. It also affects our attitude to life, how we relate to others, and our motivation for love and intimacy. My own romantic relationships have been tumultuous and I have had many disappointments, but my biggest sexual breakthrough occurred when I stopped looking externally for the ultimate relationship to make me happy. I started to accept that the love and joy I had always looked for from others could only be found inside myself.

Before I started writing this book I searched everywhere for something which reflected the work I had been doing. Although I found wonderful volumes on psychological and emotional healing, there were no practical, step-by-step guides to bringing more pleasure and inner peace into your life. My main motivation for writing this book was to share the techniques and exercises which have helped me so much. Everyone can have a happy and fulfilling sex life, beginning with yourself and then including another if you wish.

Chapter 1 will give you insights into the possible origin of your sexual issues, Chapter 2 will give you exercises to help you locate the tension and holding patterns you have in your body, and Chapter 3 will help you expand your notion of pleasure. These first three chapters will bring your psychological patterning to the surface, allowing you the clarity to do the exercises in Chapter 4 on the inner child. Chapter 5 will help you integrate these changes into a relationship and expand your eroticism with your partner, while Chapter 6 will answer the sexual questions you have always wanted to ask. Chapter 7 helps you spice up your sex life and gives you tips on the erotic adventure you have undertaken. The interviews throughout the book draw on the knowledge and experience of experts whose advice will support you in your sensual journey.

Many men and women have a lifelong struggle to be sexually happy and content. If there is one key message in this book it is that you already possess your own inner knowledge and truth, no-one else can give you the answers to your healing. All the exercises, tips and techniques in the book come from this basis and from the motto of The Pleasure Spot: "As I receive pleasure, so the whole universe receives pleasure through me."

1
You Can Go Home Again

Often people come to see me knowing they are not having the sexual fulfilment they want in their life. As they start to explore their current issue they often find the source of their problem lies in their childhood, or in an incident from long ago. Part of the process of exploring present emotional pain is to journey into our past; healing happens as a by-product of this journey. The greatest healing I have experienced is when I have decided not to stay in an emotional place that no longer works for me, and have been open to change. In this way healing can become an adventure, building up trust in yourself as you learn about who you are. This exploration alone will shift your awareness.

If we had been brought up in a culture which helped us to be in touch with our bodies and sensuality, our sexual experiences would be relaxed and joyful. At an early age we would have had a clear understanding of what turns us on, yet also understand personal boundaries. At adolescence we would be able to hold out our hand and invite another to play in this realm from a basis of communication and understanding. As very few of us have been brought up this way, this book's first step is to help you learn about connecting with yourself. When you are able to touch your own anger, frustration and disappointment, you can learn to transform these into feelings of joy, sensuality and love. If you cannot do this for yourself, you will not be able to do it with another.

I grew up with a lot of sexual repression, feeling inhibited about my body and my desires, but instead of feeling resentful I now see this childhood and adolescent period as a gift. As an adult I chose to challenge this by doing years of courses and therapy, learning to relax, having more fun, dealing with past pain. I spent many years being single, as many women have done, feeling the societal pressure to be part of a couple and searching for the ideal lover. My relationships were often a source of disappointment and unhappiness, and at times it seemed that everyone else was living happily ever after except me. In retrospect, I can see how this isolation and sense of separateness led me to have a firm sense of myself and a strong independence, which became the foundation of happier and healthier relationships. The people I know who are the most sexually alive have explored their personal creativity and sensuality without limiting themselves to what society has traditionally deemed sexual. They are able to reach out for contact with another easily, expressing love and communicating their desires clearly.

Many of the old, limited ways of defining sexuality, and outmoded ideas of what is feminine and masculine, are thankfully becoming irrelevant. It is a tragedy when what makes us feel comfortable sexually is bound by stereotypes of masculinity and femininity. These stereotypes portray men as being ready for sex at any time with anyone, and pressure them to be sexual performers and conquerors. For women the messages are that they must be sexually unassertive yet incredibly orgasmic, and be the nurturer in the sexual relationship. True sexual fulfilment comes from transcending these gender limitations, not being bound by sex roles, and being courageous enough to be sexually adventurous.

Our sexual behaviour is directly linked with the way we were treated as children. If our parents or caregivers showed us love and tenderness, then as adults we are able to express this in our sexual and emotional relationships. When a child is held, cuddled and kissed they relax and feel deep pleasure, and they build on this experience as adults. We learn in different phases and if these are not integrated then we cannot go on to the next phase of emotional development. To give us an understanding of where we are in our lives now we need to look at our past.

For many of my clients, the difficulties they are now experiencing began in their childhood. It was here that they learned to disconnect from their emotional and physical pain and first experienced feeling alone and vulnerable. The root of their sexual shame often comes from these experiences, and from receiving a message that they were somehow bad or wrong. As adults this can manifest in sexual relationships where it is almost impossible to connect lovingly with another, or feel deep personal sexual pleasure. For these people, attempts to develop intimacy bring up many old issues.

If sexual oppression and trauma are experienced in childhood, they manifest not only in our behaviour but in our body. A child who gets negative messages about masturbation often unconsciously pulls the pelvis back and tightens the genital muscles. If this stance becomes an ongoing posture, it gives the appearance of a sway-back and can cause difficulty in building up and holding sexual feelings.

Numerous studies have shown that infants who have been freely allowed to explore their bodies, including masturbation, develop motor skills and dexterity far quicker than those who have been restricted. Early toilet training can be a very traumatic event, with many children being pressured to control their bowel before they have physically developed the skills to do so. This pressure around the genitals and the associated muscle tension can lead to adult sexual problems. For men this can manifest as a lack of control over ejaculation, and for women it can be difficulty in achieving orgasm.

Bodily sexual functions are part of our existence from birth: a boy has an erection soon after birth, and a girl's vagina lubricates within the first twenty-four hours. Yet societal messages are nearly always to the contrary, with our sexuality being portrayed as suddenly hitting at puberty. It is part of a child's normal sexual development to explore and touch their body, just as they do with everything else in the external world. So a young male child who holds his penis, or a little girl who fondles herself and possibly inserts objects into her vagina are both behaving perfectly normally. Their self-exploration is laying the foundation for a relaxed and happy approach to the body, and is developing their own boundaries. When this is violated by an adult interfering with them, this normal development becomes an area of trauma.

Children who are reprimanded for masturbating will stop exploring sexual pleasure through a sense of shame, and this can impact in a major way on their future sex lives; it can be another cause of women having difficulty in reaching orgasm and men having problems with premature ejaculation and impotency. Being told, either verbally or non-verbally, that genital touch and masturbation are taboo sends the message that the genitals are "dirty" or "bad", and the child may close down to feeling in that area of their body. This manifests in an adult not feeling connected sexually and not knowing how to feel pleasure in the genitals. A child who over-masturbates or masturbates inappropriately indicates unhappiness about something in their life. They are using masturbation to comfort themselves, akin to thumb sucking, or clinging to a security blanket or toy.

INTERVIEW

DR ROBERT MACIVER, RELATIONSHIPS AND SEXUAL COUNSELLOR (BMBS, DIPLOMA 0F RACOG, DIPLOMA OF FAMILY THERAPY)

I am interested to know how people see themselves sexually, especially the stories about who they are individually, in relationship with others and in their sexual relations. I explore with people how these stories affect their lives and whether they are helpful, or detrimental and limiting. We examine together the origin of these stories, from the direct or indirect messages received in childhood and as we grew up, usually from the people most meaningful in our lives. If the messages were detrimental, they will hold the key to low self-esteem, shame, self-blame, self-criticism and self-rejection. I am trying to help people undo these stories, through questioning and examining their origins, and to help them identify the way they want their life to be.

In addressing these issues we open the door to alternative ways of thinking about sexuality and relationships, ways that could challenge the old stories, create a loophole in them. If the person is willing to look at new ways to live their life, there are ways to explore this, such as learning to interpret their behaviour from new perspectives, recognising and practising new behaviour, self-exploration and expressions of feelings.

In our society it is not all right to have sexual difficulties, yet sexuality is a normal part of life and it is important to be able to talk about and share these issues. For many men and women with feelings of shame around sexual performance, talking is a first step to healing, and to exposing the enormously powerful societal and family messages that limit and control our attitudes. Together we look at accepting body functions and desires as natural and acceptable. I help people to move away from shame and self-rejection to self-acceptance and self-love.

I recommend the Human Awareness Institute's safe workshops on relationships, love, intimacy and sexuality for anyone who has done some work on healing their sexual shame. I believe that one of their workshops is worth three months of therapy.

Only about ten percent of people are willing to look at and discuss their sexual issues, and I really think these people are courageous and need to be applauded. About seventy percent of people will have the same difficulties but have not made the first step, which is to free themselves enough to be able to speak about sexuality and its difficulties. My own biggest insights have come from learning to speak about what I feel and being able to differentiate this from feeling responsible for another's feelings. I help people to learn to ask for everything they want in a relationship and to be willing to hear and respect what the other person wants. I help them to learn not to feel shame or rejection, not to feel that they are wrong if what they want is not what someone else wants.

To do this takes real self-acceptance, and this is the key to healing our shame. Our relationships are very important in our healing; real healing occurs in the safe and accepting arms of our loving partners, when we are vulnerable enough to express what is really going on for us. This requires that we do indeed have safe and loving relationships, and if someone does not then I would encourage them to work to creating this or seek ways to find it elsewhere.

Touch was the first thing that made us feel emotionally and physically connected with our mothers. As babies it was our first sensory input and an essential part of our growth. Studies have repeatedly shown that the more a child is held, kissed and touched, the stronger and happier they are. Adult sexual behaviour often has its roots in infancy, although we have no conscious memory of it. A baby's instinctive need for nourishment causes it to suckle, and much adult eroticism is duplicated in sucking, kissing, biting, and other types of oral expression.

When a child's senses of touch, taste, sight, sound and smell have not been fully explored they will manifest in unbalanced adult sexual behaviour. Some examples of this are people who are only able to be turned on by one sense; for example, by phone sex, looking at pornography, "talking dirty", or by being drug- or alcohol-affected. Being able to use all the senses in order to be sexually aroused is very important if we want to expand our pleasure and connect with ourselves and a partner. When someone becomes obsessed with a certain way of getting turned on, or having sex, then this becomes an incredible limitation on their sexual expression. Fantasy can help arousal, but it can also take you away from your partner and the sensations in your body. If your obsession with fantasies is causing you to become distant from yourself and your partner, it removes you from pleasure sensations in your body. Often sex and intimacy become confused and we feel that the only way we can be touched and held is if we have sex.

INTERVIEW

ALAN TEGG, SEXUAL ABUSE AND TRAUMA ISSUES SPECIALIST
(Bcom, BA HONS)

The abilities to love and experience good sex are developed, they do not come naturally. They are established in the early years of life by the parents, interaction with the child, and if love and emotional generosity are not experienced by the child, then many difficulties can arise for them as adults. Until you have gained a degree of understanding and loving in the present, it will not be possible for you to have a sexually loving relationship with another.

When sexual fantasies become obsessive, they might feel good at the time but at a deeper level they hurt you because they inevitably get in the way of intimacy. If phone sex is the main way someone becomes sexually aroused, it can indicate a lack of communication in the early family environment, or a lack of intimacy and love. Phone sex duplicates a situation of little depth or real communication, because there is no bodily or eye contact and no emotional interaction.

If one of the parents was into pornography or paedophilia and this is the home atmosphere the child grows up in, this may become duplicated in negative ways. If children, rather than having a sensual joy in themselves, are exposed to abusive sexual expression, the beauty of sex gets turned into pornography, which objectifies the body, making it difficult to create intimacy and love. This can get acted out in the adult sexual field.

While it is good that sexual abuse is now being recognised as a major problem, having repercussions in adulthood, there are other forms of childhood abuse which are never acknowledged. These can involve being touched inappropriately, being denied warmth and affection, and having expressions of love returned with anger, indifference or even violence. In addition, many people come from a racial, cultural or religious background where physical closeness or emotional nurturing is not valued. If you have come from such a background, it will be difficult to naturally feel a deep sense of sexual connectedness with yourself and with another. But regardless of your childhood experiences, you can move beyond them to a place of sexual joy and fulfilment.

Adolescence and beyond

My own adolescence involved confusion about my role in society as my body changed and developed, and this impacted on my external relationships. I was moving from childhood to becoming a sexual adult and felt a lot of family tension as I challenged my parents, whose guidance I no longer wanted. Our parents give us sexual messages, even if they are not directly spoken, by the way they experience their own bodies and how they relate to each other.

The work I do now with clients often draws on going back to their adolescence, when they felt they did not fit in. If you did not bond with your same sex at this time, it becomes very difficult to move into having good relationships with the opposite sex. This is also true for lesbians and gay men, because an inability to bond with the same sex platonically will mean difficulty bonding with them in a sexual relationship. For us to heal issues around adolescence we need to be open to exploring friendships with the same sex and with the opposite sex which will nurture us.

Many deep sexual wounds are first experienced during

adolescence, often because we look for love through sex, and result from not having clear boundaries of how we should be treated and how we should treat others. Without a good primary emotional experience we will feel a sense of separateness and isolation in an intimate partnership. Intimacy is an intrinsic part of forming a good sexual relationship, along with trust and communication.

During adolescence we draw on the foundation we have experienced in childhood, and so our childhood messages become even more significant at this time because we are trying to find intimacy or love as a young adult. My adolescent peer group provided my sexual information – which more often than not was incorrect, unhelpful, and raised more questions than it answered. There was a lot of negative comparison and competition over appearance, body size, and success (or lack of success) with boys.

For most people who come to me, their first sexual experiences were not normally what they had expected. They were full of pain, trauma and misunderstanding, rather than the idealised romantic view that the media and the movies portray. We often believe that we should innately know how to have a fulfilling sexual experience, but this is rarely true for anyone. Men usually expect their first sexual relationship to be raunchy, adventurous and conquering, but if it is in fact about premature ejaculation or impotency this can give them a high level of anxiety around sex. When young women fantasise that sex will lead to everlasting love they are often disappointed to find sex a disconnecting and isolating experience. When I look back on the way I was taught about sex at school I am sad that little has changed, but there are some ground-breakers, like Samsara Tanner, who are implementing a new system.

INTERVIEW

SAMSARA TANNER, TEACHER OF PERSONAL DEVELOPMENT COURSES, INCLUDING SEX EDUCATION, TO BOYS AND GIRLS AGED SIX TO EIGHTEEN YEARS IN NSW COMMUNITY SCHOOLS

Girls in the 1990s have just as many hang-ups about menstruation and masturbation as their counterparts in the 1960s and 1970s did. While there has been a shift toward

more sexual liberation since the 1960s, there is still the same issue of shame and pressure around body images. These children's parents fell that they are more open than their parents were, but this openness does not seem to have been passed on to their children. Kids look primarily to the media for information. This becomes obvious when you teach in a classroom and you realise how little the children know. Often they have a little bit of knowledge, but areas such as fertility, sexual safety, relationship issues and personal assertiveness are frequently used out of context.

We have not been taught how to address sexuality in the classroom; people fear that it will be confrontational, so they want to avoid it. Often what is taught is left up to the head teacher, and as there is no curriculum to refer to, their own personal beliefs strongly influence what is taught. I believe sex education should be taught on a continual basis, not just left to the final years of school when it is too late to start introducing the topic of sexuality.

My teaching starts with six-year-olds and the basic question: where do babies come from? Information is given slowly, correct anatomical terms are introduced, and emotional understanding is given. I play games with the children where we use cards to work out what is appropriate and inappropriate behaviour. Questions include: What would you do if someone touched your genitals? Can you get pregnant through kissing?

My twelve-year-old students are doing projects on safe sex, puberty, contraception and fertility. This will help them deal with the traditional teenage pressures about sexuality, drugs, relationships, gay issues and sex-role stereotyping. We cannot deny that children are sexually active much earlier than most of us imagine, so it is essential that the information be given to them right throughout their schooling.

I have noticed that by the age of ten to twelve, many children have developed the attitude that their genitals are somehow wrong. They also often have negative attitudes toward menstruation, which is seen as dirty. Often I have dealt with these same children when they were younger and noticed that they were then more relaxed about their body and would admit to playing sexual games, including doctors and nurses. Twelve-year-old girls often do not know that women masturbate, as there is nothing in our culture which gives females a self-pleasuring image of their body. They also receive many messages which say that to touch themselves is a big no-no. The courses I have set up in schools provide a ground-work of education and guidance which is desperately needed.

Healing past traumas

If your first sexual experiences were negative, it is hard to build from this place a positive, loving relationship. We first need to heal these damaging early experiences. A very powerful and transforming exercise involves going back to each of your past relationships, either sexual or non-sexual, and forgiving the other person for any pain and misunderstanding which occurred between you. This will show you how much you are hanging onto from the past.

This exercise allows you to let go and move on, so that you'll be able to be more present in the here and now. It is particularly good if your past relationships ended badly or were never resolved. Often we feel that to resolve a past experience we need to be in contact with that person, and this might be impractical, impossible or inappropriate. With this exercise you are able to resolve past relationship issues regardless of whether you have any contact again with that person. The importance of this is to free us from continuing to bring our unresolved relationship issues into our present ones.

EXERCISE 1.1: LETTING THE PAST GO

Time: 20-30 minutes
Setting: Somewhere you will not be disturbed
Music: None
Lighting: Soft
Props: Paper, pencil or pen, scissors
Partner or friend: Not required

First write a list of the names of people with whom you have unresolved relationship issues. Start by sitting or lying down, closing your eyes and taking three belly breaths, placing more emphasis on the inhale than the exhale. To do a belly breath, place your hands on the belly, breathing in deeply through the nose and noticing how your belly pushes out against your hands as it fills with air. At the same time your anus should gently push out from the body. When you exhale relax back into the body. This is the method of breathing we naturally use when we are sleeping and is helpful for relaxation.

Imagine the first relationship on your list, whether it be sexual or non-sexual, and think deeply about what you need to resolve in that relationship. This can involve an emotional dialogue, expressing what was never said but needed to be, in order for you to let go. Remember what it was like when you were involved with this person, and the style of relationship you had.

The next part of the exercise you can do with your eyes open or closed. Imagine or draw a figure 8; place yourself in one of the circles and your ex-partner or past relationship in the other circle. Without judging, forgive yourself and them for the relationship not working. Recognise what was there, or not there, between you and consciously let go of the relationship. Finish by saying, "Thank you for having been in my life and for what you taught me."

Ask yourself, "Am I ready to let go?" and if the answer is yes, cut the figure 8 in half, either in your imagination or by physically cutting the paper. Separate the two circles and imagine the circle with the past relationship in it being like a balloon floating up into the atmosphere. Alternatively, physically bury, burn or let the circle go into the ocean. Know that you have retained the positive knowledge that you needed from this past relationship. Once this feels complete, allow yourself to go on to the next relationship and do the process again.

Creating healthy boundaries

Boundaries which have been taken away at an early age do not allow you to define your own space. This manifests in not being able to say no when you want to, and feeling that you have to conform to another's needs and desires, and is reflected in our inability to set our own physical, emotional and sexual limits. Here are some questions to ask yourself in order to test your boundaries:

- How close do you like to be when speaking to someone you do not know?
- How close can you physically be to someone you know well? Is

this affected by the age, gender or sexual preference of the person?
• When you do not want to do something is it easy for you to express this?
• How difficult is it for you to tell someone, verbally or non-verbally, where on your body and how you like to be touched?
• Can you discuss your needs, desires and the sort of relationship you want with another?
• Can you clearly express your interest in someone in a healthy way?
• Can you communicate clearly, verbally and non-verbally, what you do and do not want?

There is no right or wrong answer to any of the above questions, they are simply a guide to help you be clear with your sexual boundaries. As you explore the exercises, tips and techniques in this book, note whether the answers to these questions change. Often change can be subtle. To expand your security around your physical and emotional boundaries it is essential to build up trust in yourself. People who simply say yes to situations they find themselves in often feel they have little control over their life and wonder why. Being conscious of these patterns will help you set new boundaries that will work for you. Exercise 1.2 will help you to notice whether in your normal work and social environments you are able to say yes or no clearly and whether your behaviour manifests this.

EXERCISE 1.2: SETTING BOUNDARIES

Time: One day
Setting: In a work or social setting with others
Music: None
Lighting: Natural
Props: None
Partner or friend: Not required

Before you say yes or no to someone else you need to connect with yourself and find out where your limits are. At the end of the day take time for rejection and see if there is anything you would have done differently and why. Be aware of whether you said yes to things you did not want to do and the reason behind it. For example, did you allow someone to stand close to you in a way which made you feel uncomfortable? If so, think about why you did this and how you would like to assert yourself.

INTERVIEW

FLEUR BISHOP, SOCIAL WORKER AND COUNSELLOR SPECIALISING IN SEXUAL TRAUMA AND SPIRITUAL HEALING AT THE BUSH SANCTUARY HEALING AND COUNSELLING CENTRE

The model I use to help adult survivors of child sexual assault – which affects them emotionally, physiologically and physically – first covers the issue of safety. I look at external safety and how it manifests in their life, with a partner, children, family, friends, and in their living environment. Many women with histories of childhood abuse end up in relationships with a partner who is violent or has substance-abuse problems.

Safety covers practical ways to help yourself, such as locks on doors, personal alarms, mobile phones, as well as assessing the areas you travel to at night. Building up networks is important, especially for women who are single or vulnerable. For example, a single parent attending a parent and teacher night at school may feel more secure if they go with a friend When a woman is in a violent relationship but not prepared to leave it, I work on how she can feel safe within the relationship. Can she start to predict when the violence is going to come? If so, during this time she should consider staying with family or friends.

Teaching people to set boundaries is a large part of my work – helping my clients to explore where their boundaries lie and learn to say no. Children suck their thumbs as a soothing behaviour, but children who come from abusive backgrounds often learn soothing activities which are not nurturing. As adults these can manifest in self-mutilation, or developing substance abuse or eating disorders.

Many people are great at nurturing others but cannot nurture or look after themselves, yet developing good self-nurturing behaviour is essential. Something as simple as going for a walk when you feel distressed, having a hot bath, going to the beach, buying yourself something affordable – flowers, books or clothes – can all help. Many people do not know how to look after themselves when they feel low.

Another part of my work is to explore a person's belief system. I do this by getting them to imagine a circle, which represents the belief system and which contains their thoughts, behaviours and feelings. Surrounding this is the physical body. These interrelate: if the belief system is negative then the person is going to have predominantly negative feelings, thoughts and unhealthy behaviours. The physical body reflects this in headaches, gastrointestinal problems, joint aches, eye strain, high blood pressure, heart problems and even cancer. I work with the belief system, which is driving them, and move them from feeling "I am not okay" to a place of feeling "I am okay".

Your belief system can also be affected in the spiritual realm. If you were sexually assaulted as a child a set of beliefs can arise that says "God is punishing me because I don't deserve to be alive, I am not a good person." For the person to sexually heal we have to be aware of how the energy of another person has affected them, and they need to take back their physical and spiritual power.

2
Gone with the Pain

Welcome to the next part of your sensual, sexual journey. This chapter will concentrate on ways to detect your emotional blocks. It is important to acknowledge that your own individual healing will not look like anyone else's, and you also need to accept that you may slip back into your old patterns, as they have been built up over a lifetime.

Acknowledge and congratulate yourself for the depth of change you are committed to. Part of this change is accepting your truth, which comes from within and which no-one but you can give you answers. I have found that when I recognise my own negative behaviour which no longer works for me, something shifts without me doing anything. A large part of our personal growth comes from our own awareness, trusting our intuition and our bodies' sensations.

Often we find our emotional blocks buried in the debris of painful encounters. I have never met a person who has not protected themselves by burying a painful experience. We all shield ourselves in order to survive. These buried experiences manifest as physical and emotional blocks in our bodies. The motivation to detect emotional blocks usually follows a crisis, such as a death, relationship breakdown, or the inability to form a relationship – generally being in a place of emotional pain from which you want to grow. Many of my clients feel an urgency at this time to break emotional and sexual patterns that do not support what they want in their lives. Regardless of when this occurs, this deep desire to change is the first step to sexual healing. My journey has been working with my body, noticing where I feel tightness and tension and where I feel at ease. Over the years I have seen how my body has relaxed. The exercises in this chapter focus on the body work I use in my workshops and with private clients.

There are many expressions which reflect the relationship between the body and the emotions, such as "He's got a chip on his shoulder"; "She'll never stick her neck out"; "I've had a bellyful"; "He's got the whole world in his hands"; "She's such a pain in the neck", "He walks around with his nose in the air"; "She's lost her head"; "He's so hard-headed"; "My two left feet"; "He's down at heel". Parts of the body can be used as metaphors for almost any feeling. One way to expand on this is to examine our bodies as we would a map, and by studying this body map we can discover the ways we protect ourselves, hold tension and frustration, and experience pleasure. In Exercise 2.1 we use a mirror to discover the key to the map of our body.

EXERCISE 2.1: THE BODY MAP

Time: 10 minutes
Setting: Somewhere private
Music: Funky and upbeat
Lighting: Clear and bright
Props: A full-length mirror
Partner or friend: Not required

Stand naked in front of a full-length mirror in good light. Relaxing your knees, stand comfortably, close your eyes and take three deep breaths. Let go of any preconceived ideas you have about your body, including unrealistic media images of the ideal shape. Try to eliminate the usual thoughts and reactions you have to seeing yourself naked. Do not predict what you are going to see and how you are going to feel about your body. Know that each one of us is unique and perfect just as we are and we do not need to be compared to anyone else.

As you open your eyes, become aware of your shape, proportion and muscle definition. Note where your body has lines and creases. Become aware of scars, bumps or other distinguishing physical marks, and look at the upper and lower halves of the body. Do not use this examination to find faults, but as an opportunity to look at yourself closely without judgement. View the body from the side and observe the angle of the head, the neck, the shoulders and the tilt of the pelvis. Where does energy or weight reside?

The aim of the next exercise is for you to gain more awareness of your body's story and have fun exploring its history. I encourage you to go back and redo this exercise every few months, to deepen your understanding and insight into your body. Learn to appreciate and love your body and its travels.

EXERCISE 2.2: DRAWING A BODY MAP

Time: 30 minutes
Setting: Anywhere you will not be disturbed
Music: Hot Chocolate, Madonna, Aretha Franklin or any other funky music.
Lighting: Clear and bright
Props: Coloured pencils or markers, photocopy of the line drawing in this chapter or tracing paper to copy it.
Partner or friend: Not required

> Copy the line drawing on the next page on to another piece of paper, or photocopy it. Use coloured pencils to redraw the outline so that it corresponds more closely to your own shape. Colour in the parts where you hold tension, feel uncomfortable, or which have lines. When you have finished, record your insights in a journal. Why did you use certain colours on your body map? Record correlations between a specific colour and a body part. Where did you use bright or light colours, and on which parts did you use dark colours? Put in as much detail as you can and write down any insights you have in your journal, as you will use these at a later date.

Use the body map as a guide and friend to show how you feel about your body and its changes. Allow yourself to intuitively look at your body and express this on paper. An integral part of your sexual healing is trusting your own judgements about yourself and not automatically relying on others.

The body map will guide you in charting changes over a period of weeks or months. Please note that some changes, such as colour and temperature, are very subtle. When areas are cold there is very little energy, whereas warmth denotes aliveness. You may also notice a change in your stance and tightness or relaxation of muscles.

As the entire body is interconnected, holding tension in one area

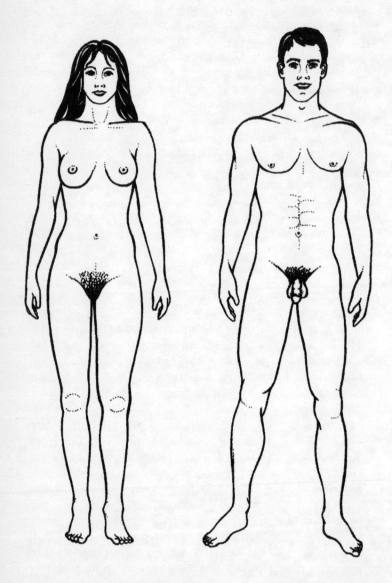

Drawing a Body Map: Copy this diagram and use it to gain more awareness of your body's story and have fun exploring its history

inevitably affects another. How we hold our bodies shows us where our tension and emotional issues are stored. There are some things we have no control over, such as aging, injuries, accidents or genetic traits. However I often see a parent and child who have very similar holding patterns in their bodies, regardless of their age. Part of this physical similarity is inherited, but I am always curious to find out whether they also have similar emotional issues which are creating the same holding patterns. These issues can include self-esteem, anger, fear, sexual trauma and repression.

When I first did a workshop on holding patterns, the participants found it hard not to criticise their bodies or judge others, but we all have holding patterns which we might believe are negative. The following tips are a guide to understanding these. There is no perfect body, and understanding holding patterns is about understanding what your body is telling you. They can help allow a tense area to become more relaxed and a blocked area a chance to heal. Do not use these tips as an excuse to criticise your body, but as a framework to expand your understanding.

TIPS: HOLDING PATTERNS

Head. The position of our head tells a lot about ourselves. If it juts out, we want to be ahead of ourselves, but often the body and feelings are left behind. Visually oriented people hold their head up, letting the eyes lead them. A head that is bent forward shows introversion, where the internal feelings predominate. Auditory people hold their heads level, listening to the sounds around them. Heads leaning to either side reflect an attitude of not being straight and up-front; in neuro-linguistic programming, if someone looks to the right they are constructing new information and if they look to the left they are remembering.

Mouth. The mouth is the part of us where we enjoy eating, talking, laughing, kissing, sucking, swallowing and biting. Because it is such an essential part of our development, it is understandable that we hold a lot of sensual, sexual feeling in this area. Holding your lips in a tight or clenched way stops you from feeling sensations and from expressing yourself. Open your mouth wide, as if you are yawning, to help you become conscious of the tensions you may be holding. Many of the people I have worked with who have experienced sexual trauma and abuse often find kissing difficult. Because the mouth and the pelvis both interact, there is a direct correlation between kissing and becoming sexually turned on.

Jaw. The position of the jaw is also indicative of our emotional patterning. A protruding jaw reflects defiance and determination, while a receding jaw indicates withheld sadness and anger. A clenched jaw is an indication of self-control, holding tension down. The mouth and jaw store much of our anger, and the boomerang exercises, later in this chapter, are designed to release tension held in the jaw.

Throat and neck. This area is the meeting point of the mind's thoughts and the body's feelings and also where we communicate vocally. When we experience pressure, conflict and confusion and do not express them, tightness, pain and restriction in the neck and throat follow. If this becomes longstanding, rigidity develops, which limits our nerves' impulses and creates tension headaches or chronic neck problems. The throat is an integral part of how we express ourselves. We can release stored-up emotion in this area through screaming, yelling, yawning, coughing and crying, and this also releases tension in the pelvis.

Shoulders. Our shoulders reveal how we express and present ourselves to the world. A scared cat raises its shoulders in readiness to protect itself. Humans react in the same way. When fear arises, these muscles tense; when fear subsides, they relax. Rounded shoulders protect the heart and constrict the chest. Retracted or pulled back shoulders are often seen when people are trying to control their emotions and their environment. I have seen extreme cases where these muscles have become locked in this holding pattern, with resulting arthritis. After prolonged periods of stress we forget how to relax our shoulders and they often stay constricted.

Arms and Hands. Our arms and hands put into action our expressions and desires. Weak, underdeveloped arms show a difficulty in reaching out and taking control of one's life, as well as powerlessness in relationships and worldly situations. As children we put our hands out to get our needs met, which is an empowering experience, but often as adults we stop doing this.

Chest. This area is central to the way in which we take in information, as well as how we absorb warmth, love and nourishment. It is the home of our heart, and our emotions and feelings originate here. It also houses our respiratory system, and those who breathe in a shallow manner will find that this affects the lungs and might manifest as nervousness or a bronchial problem. If these upper body muscles are held rigid and the abdomen is held tight, feelings are blocked off in the vulnerable abdominal region.

Abdomen. This is the most vulnerable and unprotected part of the body. It is the site of passions and emotions, and if your instinctive feeling, or "gut reaction", is blocked you may notice intestinal and colon disorders, or lower back problems. To express yourself verbally these feelings must be able to move freely up towards the head, and for them to be expressed physically and sexually they must be able to travel easily towards the pelvis.

Pelvis. This area is the foundation upon which our whole upper body rests. Tension in the neck and shoulders is often linked to tension or immobility in the pelvis. Problems arise if the pelvis is tilted too extremely in any direction. A forward, upward-tilting pelvis diminishes the natural curve of the spine, and can be accompanied by a lowering of sexual feeling. People with this pattern often have difficulty sustaining sexual feeling and it can also diminish the energy flow to the legs. A pelvis that is tilted backwards can create an unnatural curvature of the spine, and this can impede sexual release. Pelvic holding frequently originates at the time of toilet training, with control of the sphincter muscles beginning between two and three years of age. Toilet training enforced at too young an age puts physical strain on the buttocks and abdomen, as well as the anus and pelvis. Holding and straining in this area reduces the ability to relax completely. When the cheeks of your bottom have a pinched look as a result of extreme tension, there will be an over-contraction of the anal muscles and concurrent pressure on the lower back. This holding pattern ultimately limits the depth of orgasmic release.

Legs. These connect us to the feet, which ground us, allowing us to move into the world and create what we want. If your legs feel weak and ungrounded it gives a sense of feeling disempowered. When you lock your knees there is little movement in the upper body and pelvis, yet when you relax your knees movement is felt throughout the body. This makes it easier to allow emotions and feelings to flow.

Feet. As our initial and daily connection to the earth, our feet are great storytellers of our lives. Healthy, balanced feet have a slight arch and an even strength in the forward and rear parts. Feet can change with weight gain or loss, with neglect, with the tension we carry in our bodies and with the way we move. Reflexologists recognise the way in which feet reflect the interrelationship between organs and sections of the soles.

Right/Left. You will notice when looking at your body differences between the right and left sides, top and bottom, back and front. This will be reflected in weight, muscle distribution, and even the colour of the skin. The right side of the body, yang in Chinese philosophy, is associated with rational, logical thought and with expressions of assertion and authority. The left, yin in Chinese philosophy, is associated with receptivity, passivity and creativity. These sides are reflected in how we use different parts of our body. I often notice when someone cries that initially it can start from one eye, reflecting where the sadness is based.

Top/Bottom. This split is normally more pronounced than any of the others. The top half of the body is associated with extroversion, expression, communication, sight and achieving in the world. The bottom half is associated with privacy, introspection, stability and creating a home. Whatever part is proportionally larger will show a person's priority. An action oriented person might have a heavy top half of their body, while a feeling-oriented person will have a heavy bottom half of their body.

Front/Back. The front of the body represents the social self, communicating, giving and integrating with life. The back represents the receptive, unconscious part. Often muscle tension accumulates in the backs of our bodies when we do not want to deal with emotional issues.

Correlations also exist between tension held in the body and lines and creases, which indicate corresponding emotional blocks Lines across the throat, neck or jaw depict a person who had difficulty as a child expressing themselves. They were discouraged from speaking, crying or shouting. In adult life, this becomes difficulty in contacting and expressing feelings and emotions

Lines between the shoulders and arms reflect the stagnation of energy throughout the body, which may be the result of not being able to reach out for protection as a child. This manifests in adulthood as difficulty in putting thoughts into action, an inability to reach out to get what is wanted.

Lines across the chest signify a protection of the heart, and are often accompanied by rounded shoulders. A person who looks like this was not encouraged, admired, loved or appreciated enough as a child. As an adult, their breathing may be shallow, or they may suffer from low self-esteem or depression. Bronchitis, asthma or other respiratory problems may also be present.

Lines across the stomach and waist indicate a person who protects or hides their emotions. As much emotional feeling originates in this area, one way of trying to control feelings is to tighten here. This adult's breathing will not incorporate the full and proper motions of the diaphragm and belly. They may also have a weak lower back.

Lines above the pubic area reflect difficulty in allowing sexual feelings to move from the genitals to the rest of the body, while lines around the bottom reflect tension often associated with trauma during toilet training or sexual abuse. The pelvis may be tight, in which case inflexibility in dealing with others often occurs.

Getting in touch with your body

Wilhelm Reich's findings on the four stages the body goes through to orgasm – tension, charge, release and relaxation – are exaggerated in the Exercises 2.3, 2.4 and 2.5 to make sure you fully experience each one of them. As you do them in sequence you will be mirroring the orgasm cycle.

Feelings of love, sensuality and being sexually aroused all come from being in touch with our body. To get the most out of our sexual experiences it's important to build up a sexual charge in the body using breath, movement and self-expression. Sexual energy is the experience of being alive, and the methods I use are about feeling this energy throughout the body. To experience sexual joy and pleasure, deep breathing is essential.

When we are frightened we stop breathing. If we are overwhelmed by our sexual excitement we can stop these sensations by holding our breath or barely breathing. Many women who have difficulty orgasming notice that they stop breathing as their sexual feelings build, which means they stop feeling. This is usually an unconscious pattern.

For women to expand their concept of orgasmic energy they need to move away from the traditional concept of what an orgasm is. They need to relax into the body's sexually pleasurable sensations without imposing a desired outcome on themselves. For men to expand their concept of orgasmic energy they need to take the band of sexual energy which sits around the genitals and learn to pulse this sexual energy throughout the body. The emphasis is on building up a sexual charge in the body and just enjoying it, without wanting to release it as soon as possible. You are in charge of your own sexuality and in taking the emphasis away from your partner you can expand your sexual and emotional boundaries. It is important when you feel anger and frustration that you connect it to a specific tension in your body. It is very helpful if you can relate this back to a past person or experience, as this will deepen your healing.

The boomerang exercises below are from Alexander Lowen's work on bioenergetics. They are also derivations of tai chi, Taoist and yoga exercises which have been used for hundreds of years to enliven the body. My first experiences of these exercises were in group workshops in the US in the 1980s. Initially I found the positions difficult to hold and the whole process very frustrating, but at the end of the day I could not believe how alive my body felt. I was able to release a lot of my past emotional experiences, particularly anger and frustration, through these amazing exercises and I was so inspired I did a further year-long training course in bioenergetics.

Note that you may feel uncomfortable during these exercises. Your legs might shake, and during the first exercise you might feel tension in your shoulders, neck, arms and lower back. In the second exercise you will feel this in your pelvis, back or legs. It is important that you do Exercises 2.3, 2.4 and 2.5 together as a group as they reflect the orgasmic cycle.

TIPS: BOOMERANG EXERCISES

As you are doing the shoulder and pelvis exercises keep your eyes open and focus on something at eye level. Do not allow yourself to drift off into daydreaming; bring yourself back to the object you are focusing on.

While you are doing the exercises do not sway or move out of the posture until you have finished completely – this is essential to building up energy in the body.

You may need time to integrate the exercises and breathing, but if you persist you will start to experience a difference. People who already have a general level of fitness often have a quicker response.

The breath emphasis is on the inhale, as if you are breathing through a straw. The more you breathe, the more you will feel and become alive.

If you start to panic, this is an indication that you are putting more emphasis on the exhale than the inhale. It is important to relax your breathing, remain in the exercise posture, and put more emphasis on the inhale than the exhale.

Gently allow yourself to start experiencing what is beneath the surface as you say no. Expressing yourself verbally will help you release tension.

You will find that these exercises unlock emotional and

physical blocks from former experiences. If you focus on past events which have triggered your present emotional pain, you will gain great insight into your behaviour.

The more you are able to connect your anger and frustration to something concrete from childhood or adolescence, the greater the healing.

The age at which an emotion was first repressed is the age you will have to go back to, in order to allow it a healthy adult expression. If your anger was repressed as a three-year-old, then you might continue to express your anger, as an adult, like a three-year-old. This holds true for other emotions such as showing love, laughter, and the ability to cry.

The two boomerang exercises are so named because whatever tension is in your body will boomerang back on you during the exercise. Do these exercises with knees bent – this opens up the pelvis. During lovemaking, if you have your knees bent you will experience more energy flow through the body. An easy way to prove this is to stand with your knees and legs straight and try moving the pelvis – you will find very little movement. Now relax the knees and move the pelvis, and notice that there is now t a relaxation and openness in the pelvis. It is very hard to build up energy sensations of pleasure if this area is locked.

EXERCISE 2.3: THE BOOMERANG-SHOULDER

Time: 20-30 minutes to do Exercises 2.3, 2.4 and 2.5 as they are a complete set.
Setting: A room where you will not be disturbed
Music: A strong, rhythmical beat, such as African drumming, with no words
Lighting: Clear and bright
Props: None
Partner or friend: Not required

Wearing loose clothes, stand with your feet shoulder-width apart, knees relaxed. Take your arms up into the air as if you were stretching, and hold or interlace your fingers and lean back until you can feel the tension between your shoulder blades. Breathe deeply, consciously putting more emphasis on the inhale than the exhale – this charges the body with energy. If you wish to express discomfort, anger or frustration, use sounds or words such as "Ahhh", "No" or "I don't want to be here", allowing the tone of your voice to emphasise the emotions you are feeling.

Ask yourself when you have felt like this previously. Images or feelings from your childhood might arise, particularly from those times when you felt powerless. Being able to connect with the past gives us a bridge to the present. While we cannot change what happened in our childhood, we can re-address it now and become empowered and healed.

Keeping your feet shoulder-width apart and with your knees relaxed, punch the air in front of you, still breathing by placing more emphasis on the inhale than the exhale. Continue to use sounds to express yourself. Do this for two to three minutes.

Next, rotate your outstretched arms, away from the body, in full circles. Imagine you are a windmill. Do this fifteen to twenty times before progressing to the next exercise. This will allow energy to flow down the arms and open up the chest.

(a)   *(b)*   *(c)*

The Boomerang-shoulder Exercise. Whatever tension you hold in your body will boomerang back on you during the exercise. (a) Place your arms in the air, interlace your fingers and lean back. (b) Punch the air in front of you. (c) Rotate your outstretched arms.

EXERCISE 2.4: THE BOOMERANG-PELVIS

This exercise takes three to five minutes. Stand again with your feet shoulder-width apart, knees relaxed. Clench your fists and place them at your lower back, then lean your body back into them. Emphasise the in-breath, and, as with the shoulder exercise, use sounds or words to release emotions. The next part of this exercise is a release for three to five minutes. Gently letting your body hang forward, relax your arms and neck, still keeping the knees bent. Allow your breath to continue to charge the body, making sure you are still putting more emphasis on the inhale.

Be aware that following these exercises you could experience a strong tingling sensation through the hands, arms, feet and legs. Parts of the body may feel warm and there could be shaking or vibration in the legs. These are all indications that you are doing the exercises correctly.

(a)

(b)

The boomerang-pelvis Exercise: (a) Place your clenched fists on your lower back. (b) Let your body hang forward.

You might not feel this the first time you do the exercises, but only as you continue with them. If you start to experience a very uncomfortable feeling of pins and needles in the fingers, feet or mouth, this will have been caused by exhaling more than inhaling. If you start to experience this, relax the breath until the pins and needles subside, then return to breathing with more emphasis on the inhale.

After you have done Exercises 2.3 and 2.4 over a period of weeks, I encourage you to do the body map exercises (2.1 and 2.2) again and notice any changes.

EXERCISE 2.5: THE ELEPHANT DANCE

This exercise will take two to three minutes. Keeping your knees bent, walk around the room stomping your feet and being aware of the floor beneath you. With clenched fists punch the air in front of you, again using sounds or words to express yourself.

This is a wonderful exercise to feel grounded and connected with your body. At the end of each of the boomerang exercises and the elephant dance close your eyes, relax your knees, and explore the sensations which have arisen. These exercises show you where the tension in your body is located.

The Elephant Dance. Feel grounded and connected with your body. Walk around the room, stomping your feet and punching the air in front of you.

One woman I worked with found it hard to experience body sensations during our sessions. She had difficulty with the breathing techniques, but she practised these exercises at home and the next time I saw her she felt more physically comfortable. Doing the exercises again, with the proper breathing technique, she was able to have a deep body experience. She was also able to integrate the breathing techniques during lovemaking. I have seen women who have never been able to have an orgasm find that after doing these exercises they were able to change their breathing patterns enough to experience orgasm during lovemaking.

TIPS: RELEASING ANGER

Hit a cushion or bed with your fists or a tennis racquet. This gives you a feeling of physical empowerment. Use statements which support the experience, such as "No", "I hate you", "Leave me alone". Connect with the sound of your voice. Screaming is a powerful way to release tension and anger. While doing this exercise, breathe deeply to allow you to stay with the experience and connect with your body. This also releases tension in the shoulders and arms.

Lie on a bed with outstretched legs and knees, which should be straight but not stiff. Using the calf, not the heel, kick the bed rhythmically approximately a hundred times, again using statements which support the experience. This releases anger and tension in the legs.

Turning yourself on

I practised Exercise 2.6 during many workshops, gradually perfecting the movements, but did not really feel turned on or erotically charged until I also started to use my pelvic floor muscle in a series of muscular movements known as kegels. These movements do not require lots of hard work but they do require you to practise them every day. Both men and women will feel the results in two to three weeks.

You do kegels by using your pubococcygeus muscle (known as the PC muscle), which in women runs like a sling from the clitoris to anus, and in men runs from the penis to anus. You can practise locating your PC muscle by stopping yourself urinating mid-flow – the muscle you use to do this is the PC muscle.

Conditioning your PC muscle will help to sexually turn you on, and for women it has the added bonus of making orgasms stronger and longer. For men it gives greater control over ejaculation and impotence. It is recommended that both men and women exercise this muscle approximately a hundred times a day. Women do this by clenching, relaxing, pushing out and then relaxing the PC muscle. Men clench for five seconds, relax and then let go. Or both sexes, as a quicker motion, can clench, relax, clench and relax.

Doing kegels changed my whole body experience and I felt more alive and erotic as I used the breath and kegels with Exercise 2.6. When women give birth naturally, their body undulates like a wave. This movement is also reflected in women's orgasms, where there is a ripple effect which goes through the body. For men this movement is more related to the pelvis moving backward and forward, because when men experience orgasm energy is released from around the genitals. Exercise 2.6 will teach men how to create an energy experience more like a woman's orgasm. It will teach both men and women a wonderful way to turn themselves on.

TIPS: TURNING YOURSELF ON

Relax your breathing by doing belly breaths, as per Exercise 1.1. To feel turned on you need to charge the body by breathing, placing more emphasis on the inhale than exhale.

Moving your pelvis gently back and forth in a rocking motion allows the body to start to charge. As you move, use your PC muscle to do kegels.

Incorporating sounds is a wonderful way to become more sexually aroused, using sighs and delightful murmurs to express yourself. By listening to the sounds you make you can learn where your sexual energy is coming from. Deeper sounds will be coming from your genitals, while higher sounds come from your chest and head areas. Experiment and expand, expressing yourself.

Focus on the feelings in your body, using the breath to enhance these sensations.

One of my best ever workshop experiences was one dedicated to finding the inner essence. We all started by doing the wave exercise in front of an open fire. As the room became hotter, our breathing and sounds became louder and I felt my body undulate. I was very aware of the African drumming music we were listening to and I experienced a connection with the other women in the workshop. The sexual rhythm pulsed through me and I felt as if I had gone through a ritual celebration of the energy of being a woman.

EXERCISE 2.6: THE WAVE

Time: 15-20 minutes
Setting: A room or in nature
Music: Sensual, with a repeated melody
Lighting: Natural or candles
Props: None
Partner or friend: Not required, but you can do this before lovemaking with a partner

Standing with your feet shoulder-width apart and relaxing your knees, move your pelvis forward and back, as if you were making a big circle with your pubic bone. Allow your breath to make you feel as if you were charging up your body, by placing more emphasis on the inhale than exhale. Once you feel relaxed with the movement, include kegels as well. As you breathe in clench your PC muscle, and as you breathe out relax it. This will build up sexual energy in your body.

When your legs start to get tired lie down on the floor, knees bent, feet on the ground. Move the pelvis very gently backwards and forwards, being aware not to lift your bottom off the floor as this puts pressure on the lower back. Put your hand on top of your head, and as your pelvis relaxes you should feel your head moving. When women have an orgasm, the energy moves up the spine and undulates in this manner.

The movement in this exercise is the same for men and women. I often notice that when people do this exercise they still hold the pelvis tightly. The pelvis needs to be fully relaxed, by pushing into the floor. You will be able to tell if you are doing the exercise correctly because your head will move.

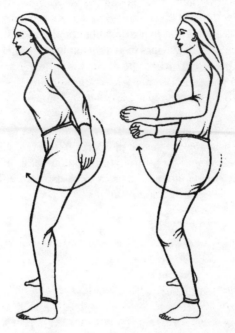

The Wave. Find your inner essence and let the sexual rhythm pulse through you. Move your pelvis forward and back, as if you were making a circle with your pubic bone.

The Wave. Lie on the floor and move your pelvis backwards and forwards. As your pelvis relaxes you should feel your head moving.

A wonderful variation of this exercise is to use a plug-in massager or vibrator on the body. Start at the top of your head, placing your hand between the massager and your head, and allow yourself to become familiar with the sensation before you remove your hand. Working down the body, massage the forehead, either side of the throat, shoulders and neck, chest, stomach, lower back, genitals, down the legs and feet. Alternatively, go for a run or a swim and when you return home do Exercise 2.6 for five minutes and finish with Exercise 2.7.

Exercise 2.7 is a technique that has been used in China and India to extend the sensation of sexual pleasure. To feel the effect you must first charge up the body through breathing and movement for approximately twenty minutes. This exercise can also be adapted and used in lovemaking or masturbation.

EXERCISE 2.7: THE ENERGY ORGASM

Time: One minute
Setting: Somewhere you will not be disturbed
Music: Ambient
Lighting: Soft
Props: None
Partner or friend: Not required, but you can do this during or after lovemaking with a partner

Lying down on the floor, with your knees bent and your feet on the floor, gently move your pelvis using kegels. As you breathe in allow your pelvis to feel turned on, and then relax. Charge up the body by doing thirty quick breaths then two deep breaths, and on the exhale breathe out with a sigh. On the last breath hold it for approximately fifteen seconds, clenching your pelvic muscles as tightly as you can, straightening your legs and pointing or flexing your toes. Let go and relax; there is no need to hold your breath longer than fifteen seconds, as you will not experience more sensations by holding your breath any longer When you feel ready, roll over onto your side and stay there for a minute before sitting up.

Frequently an emotional release is felt after this exercise, which may be expressed by crying, a feeling of sadness, or feelings of pleasure

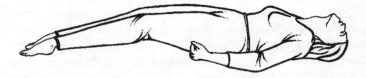

The Energy Orgasm: Clench your pelvic muscles, straighten out your legs and point your toes to extend the sensation of sexual pleasure.

and joy. For most people it is necessary to release the stored sadness first before being able to experience deep sensations of pleasure.

Once you have mastered the basics of this exercise, more advanced techniques can be incorporated. The following Taoist technique will help you feel more sensations in your body and less in your head: on your final inhalation visualise your breath coming up from your abdomen, and as you hold you breath touch your tongue to the top of your palate. As you exhale visualise the breath going down and being released through your feet.

Another variation is to imagine, on the final breath of the exercise, light coming from your perineum, up your spine to the top of the head. With your eyes closed, imagine you are looking at something between your eyebrows, and as you hold your breath place your tongue at the top of the palate and then relax. Imagine the breath being released through the belly button. You might feel a streaming of tingles throughout your body, or in your hands or arms.

People who have experienced this process after they have done Exercises 2.3-2.7 have made comments like "I remember feeling like this thirty years ago, in my childhood"; "My body experienced the most wonderful letting go, with tingles all over and I even saw different colours"; "For the first time I grieved about a loved one who died ten years ago"; and "I have had chronic back problems for years, and I can't believe my back now has no pain and I feel so relaxed".

The more relaxed you are, the easier it is for you to feel turned on.

Exercise 2.8 is a simple exercise you can do by yourself or before you start to make love. If you do this on a regular basis, you will definitely feel more sensual and calm. You need to make yourself a relaxation tape, taking yourself through each step using the script provided. Be sure to be very relaxed when you speak into the microphone because this will help you go deeper and deeper into relaxation. It is very powerful to hear your own voice guiding you through this exercise. When you make the tape, record soothing music in the background as you speak. Alternatively, a partner or friend can read the relaxation script to you while you do the exercise.

Relaxation is the key to everything we do in our life. I encourage you to incorporate this relaxation technique into your life – before you go to sleep at night, when you wake up in the morning, or anytime you feel you need a pick-me-up from the stress of life.

EXERCISE 2.8: BODY BLISS

Time: 10-15 minutes
Setting: Your bedroom
Music: Soothing and relaxing
Lighting: Low and soft
Props: A blanket in case you get cold, cassette tape and recorder to make the relaxation tape
Partner or friend: Not required, but a partner can read this section to you

Read the following into your tape (or have your partner read it to you) speaking slowly in a soothing, even tone:

"With each breath allow the body to sink deeper and deeper into relaxation as you feel your body drifting down into the bed or floor beneath you. With each breath allow yourself to relax further. Allow the ripple of relaxation to flow down through your head... your shoulders... your neck... your arms... your legs... and to your feet. See your body relaxing as you listen to the sounds around you, which are taking you deeper and deeper into relaxation. Feel the ripple of relaxation flowing through your body as if you were being lightly massaged. With each breath experience the rise and fall of your body as you breathe in and out. Just allow yourself to enjoy this feeling and give yourself time now to feel nurtured in this safe space. (Pause for a minute here.)

When you are ready, come back into your body, remembering the room around you, listening to the sounds outside, and becoming alert yet still relaxed. Stretch your body out fully, yawn, opening your eyes when you are ready, and gently roll over to one side and sit up."

Larry was in his early forties and a successful businessman when he came to see me. He had been in traditional psychotherapy for ten years, struggling to come to terms with repeated childhood sexual abuse by his mother. Any emotional or sexual intimacy brought on panic attacks and as a result he was unable to form any close, long-lasting relationships. In our weekly sessions over a period of four months, I focused on teaching him Exercises 2.3-2.7 and encouraged him to do Exercise 2.8 every day to help deal with his feelings of panic. He began to build up trust in himself and a new sense of control, and this new behaviour started to boost his level of confidence. Larry found that when he stopped practising the exercises his anxiety would return, and he realised it would take time to establish new patterns for himself. However, once he committed to regular practice he noticed a profound change and was able to establish his first close sexual relationship based on real intimacy.

Jane was in her mid-twenties and working as a designer when she came to see me, distressed because she had never had an orgasm. Although she was able to get turned on, she could not release the tension in her body through orgasm. I noted that her breathing was poor, and that as her sexual arousal escalated she would hold her breath. She also commented that her hands and feet were always cold which indicated to me that there was no energy flow to this area. I saw her for two sessions and she was able to feel warmth in her hands and feet. I taught her Exercises 2.3-2.8 and she used these techniques to achieve an orgasm. I spoke to her many months later and she said that the exercises had helped her to learn a new approach to her body and a new way to breathe. She recognised that practice was essential and that if she did not do the exercises on a regular basis she would fall back into her old patterns.

I have also run many groups with men and women on these exercises. In one women's group four of the eight participants had been going through a major life crisis because their husbands had left them for other women. These women, in their forties, still had children to raise and careers to pursue, but their sexual and emotional lives were in tatters. We spent the evening exploring breath and movement, and Exercises 2.3-2.8. After two hours of practice their faces were radiant. Each one of them felt that they had learned techniques which shifted their perspective away from their pain to their pleasure. They realised they were still sexual beings. One woman continues to visit me regularly and I was heartened to hear how the experience of that evening became the turning point in her life. She realised she could get through the pain and rejection of her broken marriage, and a year later she had formed a new, healthy relationship.

I learned Exercise 2.9 from Annie Sprinkle, an American sex educator and self-described post-porn modernist, who has done extraordinary work in the area of sexual healing, and who has specialised in bringing sexual pleasure, joy and happiness to the planet. I first did this technique as part of a women's initiation workshop. The more I practise it, the more I am able to tune into where my body feels tense and blocked, and I can then relax it and feel more pleasure. The technique is derived from Indian and Chinese practices as well as Native American (specifically the Cherokee tribe), and it supports the techniques you have become familiar with so far. It uses the same movements as Exercise 2.6 but incorporates visualisation.

EXERCISE 2.9: THE CIRCLE BREATH ORGASM

Time: 20 minutes
Setting: On the floor or on your bed
Music: Anything with a repeated, rhythmical beat
Lighting: Soft, natural
Props: None. It is important you do not use a pillow because the angle will stop the flow of breath moving through the body.
Partner or friend: Not required, but you can take this technique into lovemaking

Lie comfortably on your back, knees bent and slightly apart, and take three belly breaths. Move your pelvis gently backwards and forwards, making sure the lower back is always kept on the ground. Make small movements of 5-8 cm. Breathe evenly, either through your nose or mouth, with more emphasis on the inhale than the exhale. When you have built

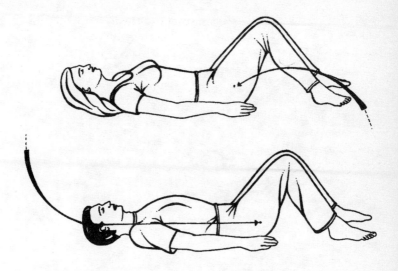

The Circle Breath Orgasm. Relax your body's tensions and feel more pleasure. Imagine a stream of light. For women, this should enter the body at the perineum; for men, it should come from the head down to the perineum.

up a rhythm, incorporate kegels. Women should imagine a stream of light entering the body at the perineum; men should imagine a stream of light coming from the head down to the perineum.

The pelvic area will start to feel warm as it becomes sexually charged with energy. Both men and women should imagine a stream of light moving in circles up through the body, stopping at intervals to energise different parts and relax any stored tension As you are moving your body, imagine light circling from the genitals up to your belly button, staying there for a few minutes then moving further up to the centre of your chest, and staying there a few more minutes. Move up to your throat, staying there a few minutes, then up to the area between your eyes, again staying there a few minutes, and finally to the top of your head. Do this a few times until you feel yourself energised. You will need to kegel, breathe, move and visualise the whole time you are doing this exercise, and you may find that you need to go back to parts of your body to charge the area up before moving on. Make deep sounds from your genitals to your belly button, and higher sounds as you

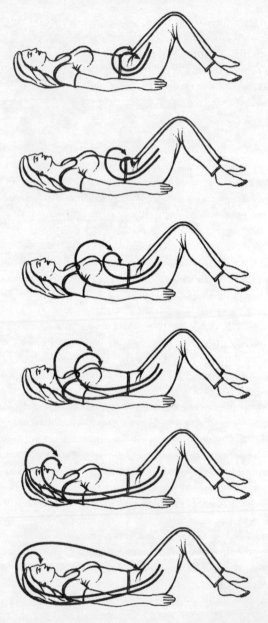

The Circle Breath Orgasm. As the pelvic area begins to feel warm, both women and men should imagine a stream of light moving in circles up the body.

move up the body to the head. This is a wonderful exercise to expand your senses and can also bring up past emotions. I have watched people laugh, cough and cry as they move through different parts of their body. Expect your body to feel different the more you do this exercise, as you clear tension from specific areas. Finish the exercise with Exercises 2.7 and 2.8.

Mary was a very orgasmic woman who was searching for a spiritual approach to her sexuality. The first time she practised Exercise 2.9 in a group setting I could see the rush of pink in her face and her body undulating as a rush of energy went through her. She told me that she felt as if there were waves of energy moving and unblocking different parts as she breathed into them. Peggy also did the exercise over a period of months, and noticed that when she got to the throat area she found it very difficult to move beyond it to the head. She felt she was choking, but she persisted, expressing through sound, coughing and crying the blocks she felt in her throat. While practising this she had an awareness that she withheld communication by not talking about the emotional issues that were important to her. With this insight something moved for her and she was able to allow feelings of pleasure to flow through her body.

If you wish to incorporate the Circle Breath orgasm in lovemaking or masturbation, be conscious of visualising circles of energy and light moving up the body as you continue to stimulate the genitals.

Many people who do the boomerang, wave and energy orgasm exercises find that what is underneath the surface for them is sadness and pain. The following exercise is one I have used many times to help people clear these feelings.

EXERCISE 2.10: TRANSFORMING SORROW TO JOY

Time: 30 minutes
Setting: Somewhere you will not be disturbed
Music: Silence, or music that you have a deep connection to
Lighting: Soft
Props: Diary to write in, paper and pens to draw
Partner or friend: Not required

Sit comfortably where you will not be disturbed. Take three

belly breaths. Allow the breath to form its own natural rhythm and bring your awareness to the middle of your chest. As you breathe in, allow yourself to feel sadness and sink deeper into what is there. Take this time to be with the depth of pain that has remained under the surface. Know that you are in a place where it is safe for you to feel whatever needs to be expressed. If you are finding this difficult, you might imagine you are expressing this to someone you care for deeply. Take this time to feel your sadness and if you need to cry do so.

In your own time start to become aware of the simple rhythms of life, the seasons changing, the phases of the moon, the progression of day and night, and nature, which is always supporting us. Allow yourself to feel this in the area of the middle of your chest; imagine the sun is shining or that there is a golden light flowing down from above you. Take this light into your body to nurture your heart and give yourself joy. During this time you might put both your hands on the chest area to help the experience and give you warmth. Imagine or feel that all the love and joy in the universe is there for you.

After this exercise keep a diary in which you express what lies beneath the surface. Use words or drawings describing your feelings and emotions. Draw on the wise part of yourself to give insight and understanding. Remember, it is very hard to find the answers outside; allow yourself to trust your inner journey.

Spend time with people who are going to nurture you, give you the space to talk about and feel the emotions which are there. Spend time in nature. Look at and appreciate the wonder it holds – the colours of the trees, the way the wind moves. Notice that nature never compares itself. It would be funny if a pine tree wanted to be a willow, or a sparrow a peacock. Each one of us is unique and with that comes our own unique journey, with its pain, laughter and growth.

Music has always been a way for people to express things very deeply; music can help you express a depth of sorrow, laughter and joy. Letting your body move to music is a wonderful way for the emotions to be expressed.

TIPS: INTEGRATING THE EXERCISE TECHNIQUES INTO YOUR LIFE

The belly breath can be used before you go into situations which are normally stressful, such as an important meeting, giving an address, asking someone on a date, or having an important intimate conversation. I always do three belly breaths to relax and centre myself before I do any media interviews, and I have often been told I come across as relaxed and natural. I also do belly breaths with my clients before beginning any counselling.

Kegeling is a great way to make yourself more animated and alive. One woman I know who does phone telemarketing uses kegels to put her final point across when she is trying to close a sales pitch.

The tips to turn yourself on are invaluable when you do not feel sexual but would like to.

Using the breathing Exercises 2.6, 2.7 and 2.9 will enable you to expand and alternate between genital orgasms and energy orgasms. Exercise 2.7 is wonderful to do with a partner, as it will allow your lovemaking sessions to go on for hours.

During lovemaking or masturbation, use sounds and visualise energy moving from the genitals to between the eyes or to the top of the head. In men this takes the emphasis off ejaculation, allowing an expansion of sensations in the body. When I have taught Exercise 2.7 to men in a group setting they have expressed wonder at having the same feelings as during ejaculation, without actually doing so. They have actually been in a room full of people breathing and not touching themselves.

INTERVIEW

HILARY ARMSTRONG, THERAPIST AND LECTURER IN CRITICAL PSYCHOLOGY AT THE UNIVERSITY OF WESTERN SYDNEY

All of my work is about breaking down the mind/body dualism and the traditional model of working with people. I think it is important for us as therapists to listen to the dominant stories people have about their histories and their body, with all its injuries and problems. It is also important to look at the alternative stories we all have, as there is always more than one story about our lives and sexual histories. My role as therapist is to work with these alternative stories. We tend to focus on the main problem story in our life, and not give much time to the alternative stories around our bodies.

I am interested in stories people have when they have felt comfortable, at ease with, or loving of themselves. I ask questions about that to start reauthoring the story about the body. I think that much of this work cannot be done in individual therapy and is best done in a supportive group atmosphere. Most life stories happen in the social sphere, so working together with others in a social atmosphere is challenging. Our culture has so many disciplinary practices which make us feel wrong if we want to pursue pleasure, and we need to challenge and move beyond this.

Healing happens in relationship to others, so therapists have to be aware of their own disciplinary practices and their own body issues. We have to be aware of and careful about labelling our clients as vulnerable or fearful or whatever, because they are always more than just this condition. The things which happen sexually for us are a metaphor for the things in the rest of our lives. You find the same processes going on in sexual interactions as are going on out in the world. A man may present as a premature ejaculator, but when you delve into his story you find that he moves in and out of relationships with great rapidity. He frequently is someone who has great difficulty conceiving of himself as staying in a relationship for any period of time.

What we do in bed is often reflected in the rest of our relationship. We need to bring awareness to this, rather than necessarily trying to change it. This is an area which can be worked on with the therapist, the group and the self. People need to learn limit setting, which occurs initially with the therapist, within a group setting, and then in a relationship. The limits which apply in bed will mirror those in the rest of the relationship. Breathing and sensate focus is also crucial – when people bring real awareness to their breathing it creates a natural body meditation.

3
Knock, Knock, Knocking on Pleasure's Door

When we imagine experiencing pleasure, we often think the answer is simple: just line up and ask for more. We all have fantasies about pleasure, but how many of us are able to put these into action? It is very common to have a lot of fear around accepting pleasure because so many mixed messages are given to us as children. We were told when we were not tired that we had to go to sleep, when we were not hungry that we had to eat, and that when we were having fun we were being naughty. The message we were receiving was that we cannot trust what we are experiencing. This is often reflected in our adult behaviour as the inner critic. The inner critic believes that we do not deserve to experience pleasure, that we are not worthy enough, not loveable enough, and the result is that we do not know how to receive pleasure from ourselves or from another.

Opening up to pleasure is the opposite of closing down through fear and anxiety. My own journey has led me to explore pleasure and sensuality by relaxing, going into myself and allowing new sensations to be felt. When we are sexually enjoying ourselves there is a deep level of inner contentment and acceptance. We can cross the bridge between sexuality and spirituality and link the two in a sexual meditation. Ancient pre-Christian Indian, Chinese and Japanese cultures all used variations of sexual techniques to commune with the Divine and create a spiritual, ecstatic state. It is very difficult to go to this place of sensual ecstasy if underneath the surface there is unexpressed anger, frustration, pain and a strong inner critic.

Expanding your senses and experiencing more pleasure can be gentle process, involving a heightened awareness of what is around you every day. When you are feeling hungry or thirsty and you finally take that first bite of tasty food or sip a cool drink, your body expands into delicious pleasure. The stimulation of the senses of taste, touch, smell, sight and sound can lead to a deeper sexual experience. The key to pleasure and our sensuality is to consciously learn to expand the senses through stretching and exercising them. This will open you to what is around you in a new way, and it is also great fun. Professional wine tasters have the same sense of taste and smell as the rest of us, but they have learned to refine and develop these senses. When we learn a new language or a musical instrument we learn to hear differently, perceiving sound and pitch in a new way. Touch becomes expanded when we learn the fundamentals of massage. When we take up photography or painting we see things in a different way: light, shade depth, dimension all take on a new, fresher perspective.

I have watched people who are happy in their body and their sensuality, and to them the many things we take for granted are an absolute delight. To these pleasurists the simple act of walking in the soft sand with their toes touching the salt water is a highly sensuous experience. For other people finding just the right fragrance for themselves can be delightful. We can all use our senses in a pleasurable form all the time. You do not have to be in a rural environment to connect with and enjoy the sensuality of the natural world. Freshly cut grass has its own sweet smell and the way the light falls through tall city buildings has its own beauty.

We often imagine that other people's sexual and sensual lives are far better than our own, but it is counter-productive to compare experiences of pleasure. We always lose out in such comparisons feeling that we are not measuring up in the pleasure stakes; there is always someone else who seems better looking, sexier or cleverer than ourselves. Sensuality is not about comparison, but about our own inner journey, which is, and must be, an individual one.

Exercise 3.1 is a wonderful way to explore the senses with a friend or partner, bringing couples closer as they expand their sense of giving and receiving. This exercise shows the depth of sensuality which is all around us and which we usually take for granted. Take time to enjoy each sense slowly and deliberately and remember that this exercise is about having fun, so make it playful. Laughter is not only allowed, it is recommended! Take your partner through the senses in any order you wish and be aware of their response as you stimulate each of them

This exercise can take people back to their childhood joy in the senses, and if past memories are triggered this can give an added insight into a particular sense These memories will be both happy and sad, but remember that the more you feel, the more you are really alive. When our senses are heightened we can more fully explore and expand them. Watch what is triggered in your mind by the smells, touches, sounds and tastes in this exercise. These sensual memories are powerful, and we can draw on them positively now as adults.

Your friend or lover should sit on cushions, or in a comfortable chair, and you need to blindfold them with a scarf or soft fabric. Surprise is the key element here, the receptive partner must not know what to expect. During the exercise you or your partner may want to make comments such as "That's nutmeg!" or "What is that?" Don't tell them what the items are and do not correct them, as this exercise is about having fun, not passing or failing a sensuality test. There are no right or wrong answers. Just enjoy and revel in each sense.

EXERCISE 3.1: DELIGHTING THE PLEASURE SENSES

Time: A morning, afternoon or evening
Setting: In nature or a room where you will not be disturbed
Music: None
Lighting: Soft
Props: Cushion or chair, blindfold
Partner or friend: Required

Collect the items from the lists below and set them on four separate trays, placing them out of sight of your partner. The lists contain my suggestions, but the more variety you have, the better. Let your imagination run wild! After your partner is blindfolded retrieve your your trays.

Olfactory stimulation: Essential oils of any kind, perfume, coffee grains, fresh bread, flowers, cough mixture, mothballs, soap, a variety of herbs and spices, furniture wax, toothpaste. Pass each item under your partner's nose, lingering just long enough for them to register each scent.

Touch stimulation: Fabrics such as silk, satin, leather, suede or fur. Ice, a feather, soft whip, loofah brush, a towel slightly warmed in a dryer or microwave. Gently touch your partner's face, arms, legs or any part of their body which is exposed, allowing them to feel all the different textures. Some people get so carried away with enjoying this sense they remove items of clothing. Let this be an added bonus for them.

Auditory stimulation: Musical instruments, a box of matches, a corked bottle, a shell you can hear the ocean in, bells, wooden sticks you can tap together, a soft whistle, a song or piece of music. Slowly take your partner through a variety of sounds, allowing slight gaps of silence between them. Let them listen to the sounds and enjoy them. You can also clap your hands, click your fingers, make sounds with your mouth (such as animal noises, kissing noises, humming, whispering), turn on a tap.

Taste stimulation: Strawberries, grapes, avocado, chocolates, cheese, champagne, wine, juice. Tease your partner with each taste by gently moving the item over their lips, almost giving them the delightful morsel, then taking it away before finally letting them enjoy it. Kissing is also a great way to stimulate this sense. If you know your partner particularly likes the taste of something make sure you add it. Avoid any unpleasant tastes.

Remove the blindfold and let your partner share what they have experienced. Swap over and ask your partner to change the order that the stimulation was given in, so you will not know what to expect. After you have finished the exercise share what you liked or disliked, remembering anything you particularly enjoyed. Which sense did you enjoy the most? If it was touch, is that a sense in your life you would like to explore further? Which sense did you enjoy the least? If sound was not as pleasurable as the other senses, perhaps you could take time to expand this sense by listening to sounds in a more conscious way. You will notice that every time you do this exercise it becomes a different sensual adventure.

Workshopping more pleasure

Over the years I have watched people in sessions and workshops search for a way to create more emotional and sexual intimacy in their lives. They have been committed to healing the pain from the past, experiencing more pleasure in the present, and unlocking the place of fear in themselves which is stopping them having the life they want. Where we hold this tension and fear in our bodies is our area of deepest vulnerability. We would all rather take the easy path to pleasure, where something or someone else will make us feel happy. Unfortunately, to explore any real depth of happiness we also have to be willing to release the pain stopping us from getting there. My courses are about having a better relationship first with yourself and then with another. One is simply not possible without the other. It sounds easy, and it should be, but lots of issues get in the way.

No single workshop will solve everyone's problems. What it can do is provide the space to be more relaxed, and to gain insights into your behaviour by allowing you to look at issues in a different light. During workshops you have the chance to crystallise the issues you have been grappling with and then change the things which no longer work for you. However, you must be aware that being in a workshop situation can give you a false sense of reality. Often the group is loving and supportive, but this may not be your daily reality. You can use the group experience as a springboard to expand your life in ways you want to but have never dared.

For example, many people are wary of approaching someone they are attracted to because they fear rejection. But whatever the outcome, an honest expression of your attraction to someone is always positive because it has moved you out of your comfort zone to a new place of challenge. Being able to express your interest in someone is incredibly liberating. If there has been a build-up of sexual tension between two people, it often just clears the air, even if nothing further happens. We often think that people must come to us, but whether your interest in someone else is accepted or rejected, having the confidence to express your feelings honestly and to accept the outcome will help dissipate the anxiety usually associated with rejection. Many of us search for a relationship to make us feel whole, and become very disillusioned and frustrated when the perfect person does not fall into our lap. When you meet someone you are attracted to and express your feelings to them, you might be pleasantly surprised at how easy it is. Honesty leads to healthy relationships, where game-playing is not the norm, and it establishes a level of intimacy from the start.

In 1991, following the Australian release of the film *Sacred Sex*, I found myself professionally organising workshops for the first time. These were called Intimacy and Love, Sacred Sex and Body, Heart and Soul, and based on the principles in the film which helped people enhance their emotional and sexual intimacy. The workshops incorporated Eastern and Western techniques of unlearning sexual shame and fear and reawakening the erotic essence.

At the first workshop, Intimacy and Love, I found myself sitting with a group of forty people ranging in age from twenty to fifty, all with varied backgrounds and life experiences, who had come to find more love and intimacy in their lives. The purpose of this two-day workshop was to introduce us to pleasure. Gary and Mary had been together for six years and had two small children. Their relationship had gone from sexual excitement and caring to anger and indifference and they wanted to heal themselves and their relationship. Andrew had issues about his bisexuality and was unsure of his sexual preference. Anna had not been in a relationship for many years and felt isolated and unfulfilled. Henry was in an unhappy marriage and was confused about whether he should leave his wife. Annette was working on issues around her sexual abuse and had closed down to any form of intimacy. One of the most profound exercises we did that weekend was on touch. We initially broke into same-sex groups where people gave and received touch. The women talked about trust, distrust, their mother and the inner feminine. The men talked about their often turbulent relationships with their fathers. At the completion of this exercise we faced the opposite-sex group, who were on the other side of the room, and slowly walked toward them, being aware of their responses. Were they angry, fearful or frustrated when they saw the opposite-sex group? Did their feelings remind them of an unresolved issue around a partner, friend, teacher or parent? This group work showed us where intimacy or love had been stopped, and the pain under the surface was acknowledged.

We then did mixed group work on touch, where everyone was fully clothed but blindfolded. We each explored other members of the group, using only touch. If a member of the group did not want to be touched, they had the option of moving away. Many women cried during and after this exercise, sharing later that they realised they had never been touched in the way they wanted. They had never been able to express their feeling of betrayal and anger about this. For some people it brought home to them that they did not know how to touch another person.

We then worked in pairs, without blindfolds, learning how to gently touch another. This exercise created an incredible shift and was profoundly healing. Comments ranged from "I have never been touched like this before, it was wonderful"; "I became aware of how I let people touch me when I don't want to be touched"; "I now feel I can be clearer about the way I want to be touched" to "I have never liked to be touched and now I know why". It gave all involved a deep insight and provoked profound reactions in all the participants.

Touch is so essential to us developing levels of pleasure, yet how many of us were adequately touched as children? Studies have shown that babies who are massaged, touched and frequently held gain weight fifty percent faster than those who are not touched. Touched babies are also more responsive and alert. Physical contact is essential to feeling happy and content. When we are attracted to someone we want to touch them and be touched by them, and when we fall in love chemicals are released in our body which contribute to the intense feelings we have for the loved one. If you could isolate these feelings and draw on them whenever you wished, you would find that pleasure in life comes from a place of love and acceptance.

People who do not like to be massaged often have a history of not being touched with sensitivity or care. For those people a level of trust needs to be established, and clear communication given about what parts of the body they do not want to be massaged. Often it is enough for those parts to be held or rocked gently, rather than massaged. Exploring pleasure means being able to relax into the sensations, so someone touching you in an unacceptable manner will stop you being able to explore new depths of bodily joy.

TIPS: TOUCH

The way you touch yourself will be the way you touch others. If you are rough or soft your partner will react by either closing down or opening up. If you are interested in how your touch is being accepted, watch and listen to the breath. If the person breathes deeply, you know they are relaxing. If they hold their breath, or tense their body, they are not enjoying the sensation and are trying to block it out.

Giving a friend or your partner a massage will help you explore touch. By relaxing yourself through a few deep breaths, you can set the pace, harmonising your breath with the other person's. On the front of the body begin by gently resting one hand in the middle of the chest and the other on the stomach or genitals. On the back of the body, place one hand between the shoulder blades and the other on the lower back. Close your eyes, and if you are standing relax your knees. Feel the rhythm of the person's breath and follow this – be conscious of harmonising your breathing throughout the massage.

Being touched alternately with silk scarves, feathers, fur, and soft suede whips will give the skin a sensual stimulus. (As they can be difficult to clean, remember to keep them away from oil, cream, lubricant or flour.)

To energise the hands before touching the body, rub them together vigorously.

Cornflour or cornstarch is a wonderful alternative to oil. It feels like silk. Gently sprinkle it over the body and use as you would a massage oil.

When touching, use the palm of your hand and follow the body's natural curves and contours. Long slow strokes feel very relaxing. Often when people start incorporating fingers into their massage it can feel to the person being massaged as though they are being poked, so ask for some feedback here. If you wish to apply pressure, do so on the recipient's exhale. Using the flat pads and palms of the hands as you lean gently into the body to apply pressure gives a wonderful sensation.

People from all cultures have for centuries used movement and dance as a way of expressing joy, pain, anger and laughter. From belly dancing to tai chi, movement has been a way of both energising and relaxing the body. Part of learning to experience pleasure is learning to read what your body says and trusting it. Exercise 3.2 will give people who are not happy with the way they dance or move a deeper understanding of why they feel that way. For people who already enjoy movement, it will develop the body's creativity further. This is a playful exercise which is not about having a fixed outcome. I have watched people change pain into ecstasy through this exercise, using the healing and transformative power of music and movement.

EXERCISE 3.1: MOVEMENT, PLEASURE AND THE ELEMENTS

Time: One-and-a-half to two hours
Setting: A room where you won't be disturbed

Music: Choose your own, or follow the music recommendations given for each element
Lighting: Natural
Props: None needed
Partner or friend: Not required

First, find some music which expresses the four elements: earth, air, fire, water. After moving to each element, draw or paint your experience, and what about this element has touched you. You might want to express something abstract, using colour or shape, or you might like to draw an image based on the places in your body where you have experienced tension or tightness. On the back of each drawing write anything which has come up for you, or use your own poetry or stories to give the pictures more meaning. What do they say to you? Look at the colours and shapes, as well as what you have written on the back, and you might see a theme or message, or realise that there is one element you might like to spend more time exploring.

Exploring music through the elements will give you more understanding of what is happening physically in your body. During the exercise it is also effective to use your voice and make sounds if appropriate

The element of earth: "Les Toreadors", *Carmen* by Bizet; *The Primitive Truth* by Brent Lewis; the theme from *2001: A Space Odyssey*; *Olatunji! Drums of Passion* by Zakir Hussain and the Rhythm Experience. Or choose your own music which has a strong base beat, such as African music, drumming, music with a tribal influence. The sounds which help you explore your feelings are deep and low. Bend your knees and let the sounds help you to move your pelvis in a gentle rocking motion. Use your feet to connect to the earth.

The element of air: "Carcarole", *Tales of Hoffmann* by Offenbach; "Spring", *The Four Seasons* by Vivaldi; *Canon* by Johann Pachelbel; "Dance of the Sugar Plum Fairy", *Nutcracker Suite* by Tchaikovsky; *Viola Concerto in G* by Georg Telemann. Music associated with this element is made by wind or string instruments. As you experience the sounds, move your upper body, torso, arms and hands. Imagine you are a reed dancing in the wind. Free your throat by making high sounds.

The element of fire: Tina Turner; The Rolling Stones; Angelique Kidjo. Choose music which is upbeat, rock'n'roll, fast Indian or Middle Eastern. Jump, gyrate, dance, really let yourself go physically and build up a sweat. Have as much Jun as possible expressing the heat within you.

The element of water: Enya; *Clair de Lune* by Debussy; *Lakme* by Delibes; *Siva Pacifica* by Anthony Copping; *Oceanic* by Vangelis. Music associated with this element is sensual, incorporating piano or soft vocals. Initially, move the whole body in flowing movements, then either sit or lie and let the music wash over you, allowing any feelings or visions to bubble up.

Exhibitionism and the exotic erotic

Feeling erotic comes from within. If I ever doubted this, it was dispelled six years ago when I did one of the most liberating and fun courses ever invented, the Sluts and Goddesses workshop. It was run by the extraordinary Annie Sprinkle and involved a group of women undertaking to explore equally the inner slut and the inner goddess. Every woman has a dormant slut and a dormant goddess within, but usually no-one wants to be the slut and everyone wants to be the goddess. The slut is the external experience of the female, whereas the goddess is the internal experience. This workshop was about uniting them, as they are really two sides of the same coin. At the end of the workshop, after we had explored each of them fully, the two were brought together to live in happy coexistence within us.

Many women remember the derisive term slut, a playground insult which came heavily loaded with negative messages about sexual promiscuity. It was a word of abuse and judgement, defining how a particular girl was seen by men and other girls. It was used to regulate how we dressed, acted, spoke, moved and where we went. This "bad girl" was rarely embraced positively, rather she was socially stigmatised. This is an example of the early sexual repression of women. The workshop gave us a way to free up this part of ourselves and own it, allowing us to be more relaxed about the aspect of female sexuality which is often viewed as shameless. Most women have seen centrefolds and been aware of the mixed messages given about these women. They are both bad for appearing naked in magazines, but also highly desirable to some men and some women. Many women feel they could never look as alluring or sexually desirable as the women they see in magazines, but in this workshop we all had the opportunity to create our own pin-up persona.

To explore our inner slut we dressed ourselves in an array of lingerie, leather, wigs, high-heels, makeup, false eyelashes, and anything else we felt would express our inner bad girl. Our props included whips, dildos, vibrators and feathers. The looks were individual and ranged from cruel dominatrix to porn star to voluptuous nymphet. We were all amazed at the transformations that took place. I was able to relax and look at my body in a new way, and to my surprise I had become the sexy woman I always longed to be. We took Polaroids of each other dressed up and in sexy, pouting poses, so that each woman could have a souvenir but be confident there were no negatives of our play. Regardless of age, size, or whether we had a disability, we had all become our own erotic stars, and we were high on a new kind of magic. The next path to discovery was exploring the goddess in ourselves. As we dressed in sensuous flowing fabric and robes there was a depth of connection amongst us. A wonderful log fire was burning and we started to breathe deeply, moving our hips to the pulsing music. Fabric and robes fell to the floor as we became hotter and hotter. It was such an empowering experience to watch a room full of beautiful women breathing and moving. It felt like an initiation into the feminine, without comparison or judgement. We shared afterwards how it had touched us deeply, interweaving all our stories, which emerged with a number of strong themes. What came up was feeling that we had not played enough in childhood and adolescence, that we were wonderful caregivers but we did not leave space for ourselves. As each woman spoke we all nodded in recognition. Fay had sexually closed down seven years ago, after the birth of her third child. This workshop was the first step in reclaiming herself. Jessica had always felt unattractive and had suffered from anorexia, Susan had been healing after an abusive relationship, and Barbara had been going through menopause and could not relate to her body. The deep bonding which took place in such a short time was incredibly healing. As I left I knew that I could build on this experience.

Although it is a number of years since I first did this workshop, the positive feelings have stayed with me. I am less judgemental of myself and others because I know that I can transform myself into a sex goddess any time I wish. You can recreate this workshop by doing Exercises 3.3 and 3.4.

EXERCISE 3.3: WOMEN'S TRANSFORMATION – THE SLUT

Time: A whole evening or afternoon to do Exercises 3.3 and 3.4
Setting: Room with one blank wall, cushions, bed or a chair
Music: Raunchy, sexy music, such as Tina Turner, Hot Chocolate, Madonna, Marvin Gaye
Lighting: Clear or natural
Props: Plain satin or other shiny fabric to be draped on a bed or chair for the photos; strong shades of red, pink, purple, or blue look good as a photographic backdrop. Polaroid camera. Clothes to dress up in, such as lingerie, wigs (these can be hired at a fancy dress shop), costume jewellery of all kinds, high-heels or boots, gloves, garter belts and stockings, boas, corsets, false eyelashes, makeup and sexy clothes. Be daring!
Partner or friend: Required

This is a great exercise to share with friends who feel like playing and having fun, but complete confidentiality is essential for it to work. Know that you do not need to use drugs or alcohol to bring out your inner bad girl, let her emerge naturally. Some women become inspired to create their slut look by exploring girlie or fetish magazines. If you do, look at the poses the models have chosen, the expressions on their faces, how they have positioned their body and what they are trying to convey. The idea is to draw out parts of yourself you have never expressed before. It is great to get dressed together, as this inspires everyone. Have one woman doing the makeup, while another helps with clothing tips, then swap so everyone gets a turn. Once everyone is dressed, encourage one another in poses which project the image you each want to convey.

Next give yourself a special slut name for your photographic session, such as Lucy Legs, Kitty, Pulsating Penny, Miss Nipples. Encourage each other to bring out a side of yourselves you did not know existed, or were too afraid to express publicly. Be provocative with the camera, flaunt parts of your body you normally hide. Do not hold back. Use the props to give an extra dimension of naughtiness. If you do not have a whip, use a belt or something else you have around the house. If you have sex toys, get them out, pose with them and include them in the photographs.

Once you have finished taking the photographs lay them out. You will be amazed at how different you all look in your new personas. Share with your friends your insights.

INTERVIEW

C. MOORE HARDY, PHOTOGRAPHER, STARFISH STUDIOS, SYDNEY

Taking photographs at Sluts and Goddesses workshops has given me the opportunity to talk to lots of women who have been recreating their inner slut. Because women need to feel completely comfortable and secure in the photos, a female photographer is best. Traditionally, "girlie" shots have been created by males, and photographing in this situation can often contain an unspoken and unwanted voyeurism, another reason why your female friends should take the photographs. When I photograph women I try to encourage and support them to feel as sexy as possible, and I like them to have the experience of being models in front of a professional photographer. All women can be photographed as sensual, sexual beings – regardless of their size, shape or age.

TIPS: C. MOORE HARDY ON TAKING EROTIC PHOTOGRAPHS

If women are concerned about their size, get them to stand side on to the camera and turn their face forward. This will make them look slimmer.

Flat-chested women can try putting rouge between the breasts and squeezing them together with the inner arms. This gives the look of a more voluptuous chest.

If women have great legs, make sure they sit down and have their legs forward in the photograph, or have them put their legs up in the air to show them off.

Photographing from above, looking down on the subject, makes them appear more petite. This also gives good breast shots.

Lying on a bed or along a couch can give you a good, long body line.

The brighter the colour, the more sexy the look, so don't wear dark colours. Reds and purples are recommended, as are lots of feather boas and jewellery. Go for an overstatement, not an understatement. This will give a raunchier look to the photographs.

The goddess is generally deemed to be beyond the reach of the average woman. She is the female who is so perfect that her beauty casts a spell over all those she comes in contact with, and her resulting power allows her to get anything she desires. She is from another world, untouchable and above our daily concerns and worries. Her hands are never dirty, she does not have undone laundry or money worries, and she is never brokenhearted (she breaks hearts). She lives in another realm.

To get inspired, look at photos of female screen idols such as Marilyn Monroe, Greta Garbo, Joan Crawford, Rita Hayworth, Elizabeth Taylor, Marlene Dietrich, Carole Lombard and Lauren Bacall. These women had an amazing presence, they were exotic, sensual, glamorous and erotic yet untouchable. They were the on-screen reflections of the mythical sensual goddesses of many cultures and religions: utterly powerful and utterly feminine. This exercise is not about comparing yourself to them, but getting some ideas for looking glamorous. If your idea of a goddess is more nature-inspired, look at photos of wilderness areas, oceans or wild rivers, and call up that female nature spirit.

Remember that the goddess is not bound by age, race, body size or physical definition. This exercise is your internal journey, where you soften the boundaries between what you imagine the goddess to be and what she really is – a part of you.

EXERCISE 3.4: WOMEN'S TRANSFORMATION – THE GODDESS

Time: An evening or afternoon
Setting: See above
Music: Sensual with a repeated melody
Lighting: Soft and muted
Props: Jewellery which represents your feminine side. Lovely but loose clothing such as a sarong or baggy dress, or soft, comfortable pants and a big T-Shirt.
Partner or friend: Required

Gather the same group of friends from Exercise 3.3 and dress together to begin to embrace the goddess. Give yourself goddess names, such as Angel, Diana, Aphrodite, Isis, Freya, Enya or Sunlove. When you are ready stand together in a circle, holding hands and admiring the physical transformations you have made. Gently let go of your hands, allowing them to fall naturally by your side, relax and slightly bend your knees, close your eyes and take three big breaths.

The next part of this exercise is the same as Exercise 2.6, which I'll repeat here for convenience. Standing with your legs shoulder width apart, relax your knees, bring your pelvis through as if you were making a big circle with your pelvic bone. Allow your breath to charge up the body, placing more emphasis on the inhale than the exhale, as if you were breathing through a straw. A feeling of pins and needles in the fingers, feet or mouth is produced through exhaling more than inhaling. If you start to experience this sensation, relax the breath until the tingles subside, then return to breathing with more emphasis on the inhale. Once you fell relaxed with the movements, include kegels, clenching your PC muscle as you breathe in and relaxing as you breathe out. This will build up the sexual energy in your body.

For the next stage of the exercise, ask everyone to turn around, facing the outside of the circle, then lie on the floor with each person's for the next stage of the exercise, ask everyone to turn around, facing the outside of the circle, then lie on the floor with each person's head pointing inwards. Bend your knees, put your feet on the ground and start to move the pelvis very gently backwards and forwards being aware not to lift the bottom of the floor as this puts pressure on the lower back. Continue to breathe and kegel as you flow with your sensual energy. A powerful way to finish this exercise is to stop the movement in the body and lake three deep breaths.

Ask each woman to connect with their creative source by visualising either a stream or wave of golden light or a current of warm energy sowing through the body. Take time to reflect on how you externalise your creative feminine energy in the world, and if applicable how you would like to change this. You could do this by nurturing yourself more, or you wish to manifest different things in your life. Allow five to ten minutes to gently come out of this sensitive space, roll onto your side in a foetal position and then sit up. When everyone is sitting make time to share your experiences. Often this workshop can give deep insights into our lives, so record this in the journal section, or by spending some quiet time reflecting on what came up for you.

Jane, a confident woman in her late forties, was working in a top corporate area and had brought up her two sons single-handedly after her husband left her. She had willingly chosen her career to be the main focus of her life, but noticed that as time went on she felt she was missing something. In her work environment she had to put aside her sexuality, describing her business meetings as "doing battle with a room full of dark suits". She attended the Sluts and Goddesses workshop, did a course on striptease, and purchased her first vibrator. I was amazed at how much she changed in a short space of time, glowing from the inside out after exploring feelings that had been dormant in her for years. She expressed them by wearing sexy underwear under her business suits, and taking more chances to meet new people and have fun.

Sandy was in her mid-twenties when she came to me concerned that her two-year relationship was going through a rocky time. She was shy and said her sexual satisfaction had become an issue between her and her partner. Initially he had been sexually attentive to her, but this had gradually changed and now sex between them contained very little foreplay. During the courses she attended, she learned techniques to improve the way she turned herself on. She was encouraged to explore masturbation for the first time and her attitude toward her body started to change, moving from trying to improve her relationship to exploring her own sexual self. Over a few months her confidence improved dramatically. I do not know whether she ultimately remained in that relationship, but she definitely appeared happier and more relaxed.

Heather a semi-retired, softly spoken and stylishly dressed woman in her mid-sixties, wanted to explore how to feel sexual. Her sex life had never been fulfilling, and after losing her husband some time before she now had the courage to explore what she felt she had always been missing. She commented on how out of touch she felt with her body and the extra weight she carried, but she religiously attended classes over a period of months, exploring breath, movement and striptease. She also bought books, erotic videos and a vibrator. After the courses finished I did not see her for about six months, and was amazed when she called in to the shop to visit. I could not believe I was looking at the same woman, she looked so happy. She had lost weight and finally found the confidence to have the facelift she had always wanted. I reflected on the woman I had met a year before and realised that it is never too late to change. Our age or our past experiences need not stand in the way of positive pleasurable growth.

Veronica Vera runs the Finishing School for Men Who Want to be Women in New York City. Men of all sexual orientations come to do her weekend courses which promote the feminine, and which she describes as "a women's studies course for men". This exercise promotes Venus energy, allowing a man to touch the inner feminine and explore being the nurturer and the object of sexual desire. Veronica says of her motivation for creating the school, "I am not interested in putting any more male energy into the world, I am much more interested in putting out female energy in the world."

Thousands of men have tried cross-dressing, either on a one-off basis or as an ongoing situation. From the football-club function to the fancy dress party, many women comment on how eager most men are to don women's clothing. There is no reason why a man should not have fun dressing up in women's clothes, as this can be a way to reveal the inner woman. There are many personas to choose from: lingerie model, librarian, glamourpuss, superslut, conservative businessperson. You can create the woman you always wanted to meet – Miss Right might be inside you rather than out there!

You can go as far as you want with this, you might like to wear lingerie but no women's clothing, or you might like to wear female clothing, but no makeup. If you have a female friend or partner who is willing to help you act out this fantasy, encourage them to help you dress up. If you do not have your own female clothing, get clothes and shoes from secondhand shops. Buy cheap makeup and experiment with it. There are specialist shops you can visit, phone or write to for catalogues of women's clothing and underwear made for men.

EXERCISE 3.5: MEN EXPLORING THE FEMININE

Time: An afternoon or evening
Setting: Somewhere you will not be disturbed
Music: Bette Midler, Barbra Streisand, Shirley Bassey, Judy Garland or Liza Minnelli
Lighting: Soft and sensual
Props: Women's clothing, wigs, make-up, scarves, costume jewellery, boa
Partner or friend: Not required

Spend time thinking about the image you want to create. You can do this by looking at women's magazines or fashion journals and considering what the feminine symbolises for you. Remember, the exercise is not just about duplicating externally what you see. You can also draw on feelings you have about your inner woman. When you choose the music, you might like to imagine a movie icon or a famous singer – this will help give you an image of what you want to create. During the time you are dressing up, close your eyes, kegel and connect with yourself. When you are fully dressed move to the music, enjoy the fabric you are wearing, and relax into the pleasure it brings you. There is no desired outcome to this exercise, it is about having fun, exploring your boundaries of the taboo, and exploring the inner feminine.

INTERVIEW

SHELLY MARS, A NEW YORK PERFORMANCE ARTIST WHO EXPLORES GENDER ISSUES, CREATES MALE PERFORMANCE CHARACTERS AND RUNS WORKSHOPS

Many years ago I started playing around with the idea of

creating male characters and called myself a "drag king" as a joke, inverting the term "drag queen". I studied men I knew by going to sex shops and sex shows, cruised Times Square and watched men on the street. I noticed how they walked, held their body, smoked a cigarette, what they did when they were nervous and when they were confident. It was fascinating and I learned a lot, which I draw on in my performances and in the classes I teach.

When I first started performing male characters I created: a sleazy male, whose sexuality I pushed to the hilt on stage. I stripped as this male character and at first many women did not know how to react. Now they appreciate that a woman is "doing" male sexuality and they have a lot of fun with it. For this very masculine character I wore a fedora hat, a suit and tie, bound my breasts down and packed something in my pants to look like male genitals. To be convincing, it was important to walk from my pelvis and keep the energy centre of the body there, which is much lower than a woman's, and to slouch a bit.

Hands are another area to be aware of: men's hands are much tenser than women's and often they are clenched. In contrast, women walk with naturally loose hands.

Obviously, women have to be aware not to stick their breasts out and to watch their voice, which must be kept low. Men's speech patterns are different from women's and it takes a lot of practice to get this right. To recreate a man it is important for women to do a lot of physical stuff, get out of their head and more into their body. Props are important: a fake moustache, facial hair and traditional male clothing will help you get into a male character.

You also need to get a sense of how that male character is feeling, and analyse what sort of man he is: what turns him on, what he eats, where he works, what music he listens to, and what his politics are. These elements vary, depending on what type of male character you are creating – a businessman is obviously quite different from a hippy. All my male characters live within myself and they come out for various reasons and at different times. Because of the performances I do, I feel I understand men more now, how they feel and what goes on in their bodies.

The art of relaxation

One of the most profound workshops I have experienced was an intensive three-month course involving relaxation, meditation and hypnotherapy. The therapists who taught us radiated ease and understanding, and my greatest discovery from that time was that real change comes from within. I realised that a deep acceptance of myself was essential to true happiness, and that the best person to help me with what I needed was myself. This understanding has become the basis of my work with others. Through deep relaxation many doors open, and I use these methods to support people in their process of change, after they have reconnected with issues from the past.

If you are upset about something you will have bodily tension around that issue, and the greater the tension, the more difficulty you will have resolving the issue. Relaxation is inextricably linked with acceptance, it allows you to step back from the problem and look at it objectively. Someone telling you to "just relax" rarely works, but using the voice to soothe and slow the pace spreads ripples of calm throughout the body and relieves tension.

Michael, an artistic and sensitive Englishman in his late twenties, came to me after trying traditional therapy to deal with a series of short, failed relationships which had left him frustrated and depressed. He said he was a wonderful giver, but always got stuck at the same stage in a relationship because he could not allow himself to feel pleasure. He complained that his body felt numb when receiving love. During our first session he was able to locate the tension in his jaw and throat and also a split in his body at the waist. This split prevented him from feeling very much below this point. He tried to practise the exercise I gave him by himself but felt the emotional pain it brought up was unbearable.

During the sessions we worked together to help him establish a gentler connection with himself, using self-relaxation, the inner child, penduling, and exaggeration – Exercises 3.6, 4.1, 4.2 and 4.4. He was able to feel connected with his body and to develop a level of trust within himself. He continued to support these new positive feelings with the relaxation techniques. In time he was able to integrate this with the body exercises and he successfully built up a new relationship with his body.

Alex, an Irish writer in his early fifties, had been exploring personal growth for many years to heal himself and unhook from his strict Catholic background. He had never felt much pleasure in his body and his main difficulty was sustaining an erection during sex. This had set up a pattern for him where he would become turned on and then worry that he would lose his erection. This caused anxiety and in turn he would lose his erection. He regularly did Exercises 2.3-2.8 and after two weeks he noticed a difference, especially that tension had been released in his jaw and neck.

To help him sustain an erection, at home he masturbated, turning himself on initially with fantasy then focusing on the feelings and sensations in his body. During this he was consciously clenching and relaxing his genital muscles. He brought himself almost to the point of orgasm, before relaxing with deep belly breathing. He did this four or five times before he came. This allowed a build-up of new sensations and feelings of pleasure around his genitals. He was able to introduce this unhurried technique into his lovemaking, staying connected with his own sensations instead of continually worrying that he would not be able to satisfy his partner.

During his sessions, we talked about the importance of communicating with his partner regarding the difficulties he was having. Being a sympathetic person, she was able to give him feedback when, due to anxiety, his breathing became shallower. He was able to change this pattern by becoming aware of her breathing and mirroring it. This helped him to become more sexually excited. He was able to reinforce these new experiences with the self-relaxation techniques, and as the new way became established his confidence increased.

We experience life through three main sensory systems: visual, auditory and kinaesthetic. To get the best results during deep relaxation exercises, use all of these. In relaxation the senses are the main way to take you deeper into yourself and relax your body. You may go to sleep during this exercise, but do not worry as the exercise will still be having a beneficial effect. Every time you practise you will find your own new, deeper level of relaxation. You can use these exercises to create loving feelings in the body, or to work on a specific issue.

If you don not deeply believe something to be true, it will not matter how many times you say it to yourself, you still will not believe it. You will learn a lot about how you feel from the reaction you have to the statements in Exercise 3.6. If a statement does not ring true, ask yourself why not. Changing the way you experience yourself requires going deeper into the experience surrounding it. The main emphasis of this technique is on assisting you to get insight into what is happening underneath your emotional exterior. Once you become familiar with the technique you can modify it, helping you to open up any areas you may wish to explore. The clearer you become about an emotional problem, the easier it will be to heal it. If you do these exercises frequently, change will come faster. To give yourself more clarity, I suggest you write out some questions or statements about areas you need to heal.

Here are some sample questions and statements.

• How can I help myself to be more connected with my body?
• What's the best way for me to relax and feel sensual?
• What would it look like, sound like and feel like if I were sexually happy?
• I worry that I am never going to be good enough. How does it look, feel and sound to have this experience?
• What would it look, sound and feel like to say, "I am good enough"?

You can replace negative statements with positive ones to help you during the relaxation exercises:

• Change "I feel empty" to "I feel fulfilled".
• Change "I am never going to get there" to "I am where I have always longed to be".
• Change "I wish I could just do it" to "I can do it".

Or you can simply take an active, positive approach to your own individual problem:

• "I am able to relax and stay connected with my body during lovemaking."
• "It is good to feel that sex is nice."
• "It is all right for me to have an orgasm."
• "It is all right for me to have an erection."
• "I am able to stay relaxed during sex."
• "I know I can communicate with my partner about my sexual problem."

EXERCISE 3.6: SELF-RELAXATION

Time: 30 minutes
Setting: Somewhere you will not be disturbed
Music: Ambient
Lighting: Soft
Props: None
Partner or friend: Not required

Sit or lie comfortably, with your back supported by a chair, mattress or the floor. Remove or loosen any clothing which is restricting you. Place your hands by your side and have your legs uncrossed (crossed arms or legs can become heavy and uncomfortable when you are in a deeply relaxed position). Close your eyes and take a few deep breaths.

Use the script below as a guide. Read it until you are familiar with it and can repeat it to yourself. Once you become familiar with it make up an audio tape using your voice and soft background music. Listening to your own voice on tape can be a very powerful experience. You can add to the existing script, or make up your own, but remember that it is important to include visual, auditory and kinaesthetic components. Speak in a slow, calm voice on tape. The more relaxed your voice is, the more easily you will sink into relaxation. If you decide to do these exercises with someone reading the text to you, make sure they are very aware of the pace you want to work at. Indicate when you are ready to move on either verbally, by saying "yes" out loud, or indicate to them by moving a finger.

"Allow yourself to take three big breaths, just letting go with each exhale. Become aware of any sounds around you, just letting them float in and out as you feel your body relaxing with each breath. Letting your body find its own natural rhythm now, letting go of the outside world as you move deeper and deeper into your style of relaxation, knowing you can adjust your body at any time to become more comfortable. And just as you can focus on your body now, letting yourself feel as if any tension in your body is being lightly massaged, moving up into the cool warmth as you let yourself go. Seeing any tension in your body dissolving, move on down into the body, remembering how it feels to relax, taking this time to hear any sound, going deeper and deeper.

"See how many muscles you can now let go of, watch the rise and fall of each breath, letting go into the comfort which is beneath you and all around you. So you can learn how to go deeper and deeper, I am going to count down from five to one, and with each number you can float into your own depth of relaxation.

"5. Going deeper and deeper into the stillness...

4. Drifting on down to...

3. Fading away into the silence of inside...

2. Deeper and deeper...

1. And going deeper with each breath out...

"Find a special place inside you; it could be a garden, a beach, a room, or any other place which has a unique or magical quality. Allow yourself to become aware of the feelings and sounds associated with this place. You may notice how things look, the colours and the interplay of light, just take this time to experience everything fully. In this space you may find a person who is your inner guide or healer, the part of you who has wisdom and knowledge. Allow this person to stay close to you so you can connect with them when needed. When you are ready explore an area of your life of which you would like to have more understanding. In your own time, take yourself back to where this problem is occurring and visualise a specific situation."

[Insert your own relevant issue here, such as "When I lose my erection...", "When I cannot relax and have an orgasm..." or "When I become fearful of touch...".] Now remember the problem selected.

"Go back to a situation where this problem is occurring in your life. Where were you and what was happening? Can you see yourself in this situation? What are you doing or feeling? Can you hear anything? Really allow yourself time to experience this. Locate where in your physical body you feel this, as you think of the problem. Are there feelings of moving out of the physical body?

Where is the energy located? Describe this to yourself or out loud, breathing into the sensations and not doing anything, just watching whatever happens.

"Does the issue you have connected with have a shape or size, a colour or texture, a depth or contrast? Is it in the front of your body, the back or throughout? Does it have a sound, vibration, melody, rhythm or tempo? Can you hear it in both ears or only one? Is it moving or still? Is it light or heavy? Does it have a texture or weight? Does it have a direction? Is it hot or cold, is it shiny or flat? It's important to keep repeating these questions over to yourself, until you experience a change. You can take this time to give yourself any guidance which will help you with the issue. Keep breathing into it and watch anything that happens. Rest quietly for a few minutes and when you are ready take three deep breaths.

"In a moment, I am going to count from one to five and you will return to normal waking consciousness. Remember, you can bring back with you anything from this time inside, returning easily to this state of relaxation and comfort whenever you wish. Know that you can draw on this whenever you need to, in the night when you dream, or in the day-to-day workings of your unconscious mind.

[Increase the cadence and tempo of your voice.]

'1. Readying yourself to be alert and awake.

2. Taking a deep breath, move your fingers and toes.

3. Coming back to the room more and more with each breath.

4. Breathing in freshness and aliveness.

5. Coming back to normal waking consciousness, stretching your body, taking a big yawn and letting your eyes open." When you have finished the exercise, spend some quiet time by yourself and later use a journal to write about your experience.

Warwick was in his late forties and had always suffered from impotence. He came to see me because he wanted to resolve this issue. Before I got him to do the relaxation techniques he verbalised some statements to help his process of change: "I am able to sustain an erection"; "When I am in a sexual situation I am able to relax and stay with the sensations in my body"; "It is wonderful to feel sexual pleasure"; "I know I can communicate easily with my partner about what's happening with me sexually"; "It is all right whether I have an erection or not". When he was in a place of deep relaxation, I slowly read these statements back to him, giving him time to notice any reaction he had to them.

Warwick realised that his difficulty with impotence was due to his problems with intimacy. He felt that showing affection, other than in a purely sexual context, would give his partner the misconception that he was committed to the relationship. Holding hands, kissing, cuddling and communicating how much he cared for his partner were not part of his normal behaviour. I explained to him that whether you are with someone for five minutes, one month or twenty years, it is very difficult to experience a level of emotional intimacy if you are judging whether they are the right person to spend the rest of your life with or not. Warwick was able to go on to create a deeper relationship with his partner, resulting in a relaxation around the issue of impotence.

Claudia was in her late twenties and had come to an Energy and Breath Orgasm workshop where she learned Exercises 2.3-2.8. Through these exercises she was able to realise that as her sexual feelings escalated, at a certain point she would hold her breath. This is a very common problem for many women. As sexual sensations build up in the body and reach a certain level, there is a fear that the feelings are too much, and many women stop them either by shallow breathing or holding their breath.

Claudia was able to change her breathing pattern, but she still wanted to feel more relaxed during lovemaking and to develop her sensual self. We explored Exercise 3.6 and she focused on two statements which kept coming up for her: "I am bad when I feel pleasure" and "I feel a lot of shame around my body". She was able to locate emotional pain in her belly and chest, which led her back to a childhood trauma where she had been caught masturbating and told that she was bad. She had been brought up by her single mother, who rarely held or touched her in a loving way, and she had found showing any affection towards others as an adult difficult. By going into the experience, describing what she saw, felt and heard, it shifted.

Maurice came to see me when he was in his late twenties, concerned that every time he was in a sexual situation, especially kissing someone he was attracted to, he started to panic. He became very fearful, breathing rapidly and not knowing what to do but move away from his partner. We located this anxiety as being caused by the sexual abuse he had suffered as a child, which had always started with kissing. Maurice had explored various therapies but was still not able to develop an intimate relationship

During our sessions he learned the self-relaxation technique, which he then used prior to situations likely to cause anxiety. He focused on seeing and feeling himself relaxed as he kissed his partner; reminding himself that

He was an adult now, able to actively participate in sexual situations. This replaced his earlier picture of himself as being overwhelmed by another's sexual advances toward him. As he was able to get a distance from his childhood abuse, Maurice noticed he had more confidence and less fear. He also saw that if he did not practise the exercises he slipped back into feeling slightly anxious, though nothing like he had earlier.

The next exercise is on age regression. Age regression can help you understand past patterns, such as frequent illnesses without a physical cause, fear, shame and insecurity. During this exercise you will go back in time, first focusing on a recent situation, then going back to about ten years ago, then back to about twenty years ago (depending on your age), then to your life as a child, remembering the first time you experienced this feeling in this lifetime (see the diagram below). This process can be very intense; you may need to seek out a good therapist to support you in handling past memories and emotions. As this is a very powerful exercise, give yourself time to integrate your experience and spend some quiet time reflecting on what you have been through. Record your feelings in a journal.

EXERCISE 3.7: AGE REGRESSION

Time: Approximately one hour
Setting: Somewhere you will not be disturbed
Music: Ambient
Lighting: Soft, natural
Props: None needed
Partner or friend: Not required

Start by imagining a long corridor with many doors, each leading back in time. At the end of the corridor is a bright light. You will be stopping at each door as you go back to an earlier age. Focus on the problem you wish to deal with – the more specific you can be the better.

Remember a recent situation when you had this problem, recall the feeling and where this is located in your body. Allow time for your senses to adjust, seeing what is around you, connecting with your feelings and hearing anything in this situation.

When you are ready, take a few deep breaths and start to move through the corridor of time back to an earlier time, towards the bright light. Stand in front of the first door, feeling what it is like. When you open the door you will find yourself moving back about ten years. Become aware of what is around you and in your own time see what is there. Can you hear anything? What are you feeling?

When you are ready, continue back in time, moving down the corridor towards the bright light, to a time twenty years ago. Stand in front of the next door, take a few deep breaths and open the door. Allow yourself to fully experience this situation, seeing what is around you and becoming aware of any sounds and sensations. In your own time move back to the corridor, down towards the light until you reach the next door.

As you step through the door now you will find yourself as a child. You will see yourself in the body of a child, with very small arms and legs. Listen as a child, feeling through the tender heart of a little girl or boy. Describe, out loud if you wish, where you are, whether you are alone or with others. Allow yourself to express how you are feeling. As you take a few deep breaths, become aware of any sounds around you and connect with your feelings. Allow yourself time in this experience.

When you are ready, bring in the light which was in the corridor, or the sunlight of a beautiful spring day, and let this light spread through the years and all the past situations you have relived Relax and enjoy this healing. If you wish you can allow your adult self to hold your child and heal the past wounds. (For more understanding of the inner child and adult connection, see Chapter 4.)

With this new understanding, imagine yourself in the future in the same situation which in the past would have evoked painful feelings Now you can breathe more fully, and the pain has subsided or even disappeared. Remember this and allow your awareness to expand. If you wish, describe aloud how

this feels. Become aware of any sounds or anything you see.
When you are ready:

• prepare yourself to be alert and awake
• take a deep breath, move your fingers and toes
• come back to the room more and more with each breath, breathing in freshness and aliveness
• come back to normal waking consciousness by stretching your body, taking a big yawn and letting your eyes open.

Remember you can bring back with you into the present anything from this future time and you can return easily to this state of relaxation and comfort whenever you wish. Know that you can draw on this whenever you need to, in the night when you dream, or in your unconscious mind.

INTERVIEW

KEVIN OLVER, PSYCHOLOGIST AND CLINICAL HYPNOTHERAPIST, AND A SPECIALIST IN THE FIELD OF HUMAN CONSCIOUSNESS. HE LECTURES AND TRAINS WIDELY THROUGHOUT AUSTRALIA, USA AND THE UK.

Relaxation is the foundation of all healing because when we are able to relax we can step back from our problems, whether they be physical difficulties, mental tension or emotional anguish. As soon as relaxation happens, we have distance from the pain which is the key to healing and wholeness. The business of the mind is like weeds in the garden of the being, and it is essential to allow time to tend to the mind's garden. To be able to relax, even for a half-hour each day, allows us to transform the wilderness of the mind into the garden of the heart, a place where it is possible to enjoy life with playfulness and consciousness.

This relaxation will spread throughout the rest of the day l but you need to make a commitment to yourself to do this. It is essential in the process of being whole. This is where freedom lies, in the absolute truth and relaxation of who one really is. Relaxation techniques will help you when strong

emotions come up, and during times of difficulty and challenge. When your emotions are too strong to handle, or situations are too challenging, then it is not a time to stop but to seek out the help of a good therapist who can support you.

4

In the Home of the Senses:
Integrating New Ways of Being into
Everyday Life

Many people have emotional patterns which recur regularly in their lives and become a block to the positive change they wish to make. This chapter deals with the inner child, an understanding of which will let you see where many of these blocks are and help you to shift them. The term "inner child" has been used in many ways and has come to mean different things to different people. To me the inner child is four years old and symbolises the part of myself which still retains a childlike quality. It is a reflection of the relationship you experienced with your parents, siblings and major caregivers. This part of you that still wants to be loved and protected. Fear and insecurity are its main concerns.

So much of our healing depends on how we relate to the world. Our world view is set at a very young age and much of our adult behaviour is drawn from this child's perspective. As babies we were totally dependent on the adults around us for care and love; our survival literally depended on them. So we became acutely aware of our parents' or primary caregivers' moods, and whether they came when we cried, enjoyed holding us, talked to to us and touched us. We learned how to influence their behaviour to try to get our needs met. Becoming very flexible, we learned to adjust to different circumstances and develop various strategies to get an adult's attention. As we grew older and had to deal with different situations and people these strategies became more complex.

Our first experience of something is very powerful: from feeling rain, to touching a flower to receiving a slap. As young children we were like sponges, absorbing everything around us, and by four years of age our way of relating in the world had been set. Our fears and desires had been established; we had decided how to behave, and whether we were loveable, assertive, shy or trusting. The basic personality was set. This can later change superficially, but does not change on a deep level unless you work on developing insight into the childlike strategies you have established. These are part of your personality, part of your internal defence system, and you use them to stay alive. As a child these strategies worked positively, enabling you to get what you wanted from a mother, father or sibling. Now, as an adult, they are probably less useful to you, yet you might still be allowing them to run your life.

An example of these childlike strategies is saying yes to things we do not want to do because we want people to like us. How often do you automatically agree to do something and then later regret it? The underlying strategy of a four-year-old is that if people like us they will spend time with us and take care of us. In reality, you are now an adult who can look after yourself, and yet the inner child still believes they need someone to look after them, as all young children do.

We also draw on other personality strategies – humour, anger, independence or not showing our emotions – to make people respond to us and to get what we want. For us to become aware of our strategies and discard those which have become detrimental to us as adults, we have to look to our past and see how it affects our present life.

All our experiences from the past become memories, just like old photos or movies prompt us to remember a time which is over. These memories are kept in our unconscious mind, which is like a big computer storing millions of pieces of data. A photo is evidence of a moment which was present but no longer exists, and we have millions of these photos in our mind. These are harmless, but we often live our lives as if these photos or movies are still happening now. Fearful memories are repressed because they are too frightening to deal with. Although they are not real, are just a memory fragment, if you repress them you keep them alive by reacting to them. The unconscious mind cannot tell the difference between an old photo, an old movie and current reality, and you react emotionally and physically in the same way to all of them. Your inner child represses terrifying memories to protect you because it believes them still to be real.

The techniques and exercises in this chapter will give you a foundation to clear away the old photos and movies, enabling you to see, hear and feel more from your current reality than from the past. They will give you a way to deal with the underlying fear of the inner child and replace it with a sense of peace. From this new place you will have a fresh perspective and can learn to live in the moment.

If you lived with your old photos out, or home movies running all the time, you would be living out of a dream, believing that you were still a child and acting accordingly. If an old photo or movie is hurting you now, it is because to you it is still alive, and many of the things you are afraid of are these old memories. Many of them are based on self-criticism and comparison: "I'm ugly;" "I'm not good enough", "I'm not sexy" or "I'm not smart enough". The memories will always be there, but we do not have to live our lives through them. If you have experienced emotional and sexual trauma in your past, you do not have to re-experience it in your sexual life now. To be able to move on from this past trauma is essential. You can be healed and can learn to build up an emotional trust in yourself. You will start to live in the here and now, with all the love and caring you deserve, free of the pain of the past.

The mind's main function is to protect the body; it is part of the defence system and so it worries about survival. However, much of our thinking and planning about the future is a projection from the past. If we believe our survival is threatened we can panic: I don't know whether I am going to have enough money to pay the rent, and if I don't pay the rent then I will not have anywhere to live – I will have to live on the street. In reality it might be that the rent is paid a day late, but the mind has created a very stressful situation and projected the worst possible scenario, one which is not based on reality.

Not only will the mind protect the body, but it can also cause the body to become ill. If you were normally a conscientious student but at some time you were unable to complete a project, you might have made yourself sick with worry. When as an adult a similarly stressful situation arises, you can unconsciously fall back on this same strategy and become physically ill. Your inner child is fearful and can cause you to develop a minor physical ailment in order to "save" you from a difficult situation. If as a child, you had an issue about your body, then this flows into the area of your adult sexuality.

I recently counselled a man who as a child had an underdeveloped testicle and he still felt a lot of shame around his genitals, even though as an adult the problem had been rectified. His inner child still believed there was something wrong with him, and this was affecting him sexually as an adult.

I did a three-month residential course on exploring the inner child in the USA in the early 1980s and it was an experience which transformed my life. It gave me a whole new understanding of who I am and it is something I still draw on many years later. This chapter is based on many of the helpful techniques I learned and the insights I gained.

Childhood Conditioning

In our childhood our behaviour was directed. We were told, "Don't do that"; "Good children do this"; "Only do it this way". We decided at an early age whether we wanted to accept these statements or not. Around three to four years of age you start asserting yourself and saying no to these messages, either verbally or non-verbally. (Behaviour such as temper-tantrums, refusing to do what has been asked are non-verbal examples.)

When you take for granted the messages around you, this becomes hidden conditioning. If you grew up in a household where everything was orderly and neat, you take for granted that this is normal. There is also a type of underlying conditioning which develops when we get the message that "our type" never make it to the top, or it's unmasculine to show your feelings, or that women never enjoy sex. This is often not expressed directly, but it strongly influences the strategies we develop. Cultural or religious conditioning is also powerful – it can teach you not to touch others, that it is unacceptable to stand close to other people, that women need protection, or that there is an acceptable and unacceptable way to dress.

All these types of childhood conditioning become reflected in our sex lives and our close personal relationships. If your parents had a relationship where there was little affection or communication, then this is what you will believe relationships to be. As an adult, when you develop your own intimate relationships, you will often mirror this first relationship pattern. If your conditioning is not to talk about your feelings to a partner, then the idea of expressing your emotions to the person you love will be alien to you. If a culture decrees that men must always make the first move, or that it is unladylike to be assertive and strong, then women will be doubly restricted in their ability to express their interest in someone. Men brought up with these beliefs can find it very stressful approaching someone, as the fear of rejection is intense, yet they know they must always be the ones to make the first move.

We do not learn in our school environment how to form intimate, close relationships. There we were subject to peer-group pressure, which was both seductive and ruthless. While it made us feel part of a group, it was also characterised by malicious gossip, a difficulty in expressing our true selves (especially if we were different from the group), and a betrayal of trust. Peer-group pressure can cause sexual and emotional alienation and can be a place of competition and judgement. Our peer-group conditioning teaches us how to relate to the same sex and to the opposite sex. If our adolescent peer experiences with the same sex are only negative, we find it difficult to bond.

We are all expected to know how to relate in relationships with the same and opposite sex, but if you have never felt that you could relate or empathise then you will always feel like an outsider. It is important, regardless of who we bond with as adults, to bond with our own sex in adolescence. This is how we learn to feel we belong to our gender. Unfortunately in our society we have very few same-sex rites of passage to help us develop a depth of understanding of either the feminine or masculine in order to nurture and support one another.

In social settings competitiveness between the same sex is common, yet it diminishes everybody's sense of self-esteem. Instead of accepting yourself just as you are, you can get caught in a vicious cycle of feeling you are not good-looking enough, entertaining enough or desirable enough. The emotionally healthy alternative is to look for a connection with others in a place of equality – not seeing others as better or worse than yourself, just different. In this way you make a friend and an ally, not a competitor.

When you look for a partner, you tend to look either for the qualities of your mother or father, or for qualities which are exactly the opposite. Ironically, even though you may look for the opposite traits, you often end up with a partner whose emotional patterns duplicate the dynamics of your parents. You can also unconsciously develop many of your parents' traits. I was at a party recently and bumped into a friend I had not seen for many years. When I remarked that I could not believe how much he looked and acted like his father he reacted angrily, denying any similarity. While it is often difficult for us see the traits of our parents in ourselves, it is often easy for others to see them.

Desires and fears

All of our current desires come from the past. They are based in us trying, in the present, to satisfy something unfulfilled from our child-hood. These desires are connected to yet older desires. It is like a tree which has branches from which other branches grow and each branch has leaves. They are all attached to one another and just like the tree everything goes back to the root-need to survive. A desire is the same as a fear, but a desire is expressed in a positive way and a fear is expressed in a negative way. The desire to be really beautiful comes from the fear of being unattractive. Every desire comes from an expression of dissatisfaction, which often comes from comparing yourself to others. The way to make big changes in your life is to realise what is behind your desires.

Stephanie in her late twenties had just finished a painful, seven-year marriage and wanted to find a new partner to take care of her. Initially she visited the shop looking for information on how to be the best lover possible, but over the course of a year she participated in many of my women's workshops. The change in her was remarkable and she was able to move from searching externally for love to looking within. Recently she sent me a card expressing joy in finding inside her "a beautiful woman". Instead of her inner child looking for someone to take care of her, she had decided to love and nurture herself, and not to look for a partner to do this for her. In doing so her adult self became empowered. We all search for someone else to love us, but when we enable our inner child and adult to both nurture one another, then there is a feeling of deep emotional completion. At this point of centredness and clarity we do not need to look externally for a loving relationship because we already have one with ourselves. We can then enjoy the blessing of a relationship with another, should one come along, because we are not coming from a position of neediness. Women in particular need to heal from the destructive belief that they need someone else to look after them, or that they need someone else for their own emotional survival. When we look externally for sexual approval, we always lose. A lover can tell us we are sexually desirable, but if we do not love and feel turned on to our own body the appreciative comment will be meaningless. Our self-esteem can be tied up with this notion, and so when we are not sexually desirable to a lover anymore this can create feelings of abandonment, inadequacy and self-hatred. Annie Sprinkle has put this so well: "I never feel needful of sex, because I have learned how to nourish myself with feelings of desire. I know that I am the source of my own pleasure and others simply add to it."

Ironically, a major component of fear is actually fear of the positive. We all search for love, joy and success, but often when we find it we sabotage our own happiness. In childhood when we were enjoying ourselves and blossoming, school, religion and the adults around us often restricted our growth, telling us we were making too much noise or running around too much, or not to touch ourselves like that. This happened in so many situations, we learned that when we felt ourselves expanding this was not acceptable. As adults the feeling of expansion is tied up with experiencing the unknown, which can put the inner child in an uncomfortable place.

All the personal strategies you have developed are based on searching for love and approval. Sometimes you find love but do not know what to do with it, or believe that you do not deserve to be loved. Or you find approval when someone says something nice to you, but because you are unable to accept it you respond negatively. When you are complimented do you say to yourself, "If they only knew me better they would never say that". If you receive a compliment about your appearance is your automatic reaction to say, "No, I feel really fat today"? The reverse situation often has the same root problem. We all know people who constantly tell us how great they are, but this really masks a deep insecurity about themselves.

Many people put so much time and energy into finding someone to love, yet when they find a partner they spend an inordinate amount of time worrying about the relationship. Self-defeating statements such as "I don't know what they see in me"; "Will this relationship last or fall apart like all the others?"; "They will probably meet someone else and leave me" always cause us pain. These negative thought patterns will not help establish the intimacy you desire, they will push your partner away from you.

The reason we are often fearful when we love someone is because our inner child fears that this person, whom our four-year-old believes we need to look after us, might abandon us. The fear that if this adult leaves us our survival will be threatened can easily be projected onto the partner, who in the inner child's eyes is the adult in the relationship. We often sabotage our life. We might want to do something but we create a situation where it is not possible; we want to go for a holiday to the beach but our inner child is scared of big waves, so when we pack, it is for a skiing holiday. Unpacking at the holiday destination we cannot understand how we could have got it so wrong, but it is because our four-year-old has sabotaged this situation. Or we might really want to go to a film with a friend, but we have spent so long getting ready or doing household chores that it is too late to go. Again the inner child has sabotaged things.

The following exercises are designed to explore your inner child and to understand why you have established particular patterns. You can do these exercises singly or in combination, and I encourage you to try them all and incorporate them regularly into your life.

I recommend that you do Exercise 4.1 when you first wake in the morning and before you go to bed at night. Its purpose is to allow you to go deeper into yourself and to learn what motivates your behaviour. I used this technique every day for three months, and I felt much more in touch with what was emotionally behind my decisions. When we see clearly what creates conflict between our adult and inner child we are able to pinpoint why we get into inexplicable bad moods, feel frustrated or confused for no apparent reason. I resolved these issues in my own life by going deeply into whatever feeling I was experiencing and taking it back to what had happened during the day, or even in the past ten minutes. I was often surprised at where my feelings came from; something which had seemed unimportant at the time had actually affected my inner child significantly. For example, I might have been looking forward to seeing a friend and they cancelled at the last minute, leaving my inner child feeling hurt and rejected. In reality the situation may have arisen because of an emergency in the friend's life, so as an adult I would talk to my inner child and reassure her until I felt calm and safe.

Establishing a rapport with your inner child is essential, but it is important when you are doing these exercises to start and finish the process as an adult. Use your senses to connect to everything around you – being in the here and now brings you back to the adult. Never try to dominate the inner child, and try to be understanding rather than becoming angry. Speak to the inner child as you would to a dear friend. Much of the time the inner child is angry, frustrated or sad because no-one is listening or emotionally empathising with them. What is your inner child worried about today? Remember that your problems are based on the desires, fears and strategies of a four-year-old. The questions you ask must be clear, not vague or ambiguous, and it is best to write them out beforehand. Sometimes you may need to refer back to these questions over a period of months.

EXERCISE 4.1: INTUITIVE DIALOGUE – THE INNER CHILD TALKING TO THE ADULT

Time: 10-15 minutes
Setting: A room where you will not be disturbed
Music: None
Lighting: Soft
Props: Two cushions
Partner or friend: Not required

Start by placing the two cushions on the floor facing each other. Sit on one of the cushions, close your eyes and imagine your inner child is sitting on the cushion in front of you. If you were given a nickname as a child, use this name when speaking to the inner child Have a conversation with your inner child, which might run something like this:

ADULT: How are you feeling today?

CHILD: I am not feeling happy, I am really worried because...

ADULT: What do you need from me right now?

CHILD: I need you to...

ADULT: Know that I will be there for you, to help you through this situation.

CHILD: But I am still unhappy about...

ADULT: I understand you and want you to remember you are not alone. I will be there for you.

CHILD: I feel happier about this because I know you will be there to help me.

ADULT: I love you and I will always be there for you.

At the end of the exercise give your inner child a hug, either by putting your arms around yourself or by hugging the cushion the child has been sitting on. Once you become relaxed with this kind of intuitive dialogue use it daily to check in with what is happening with your inner child. Often just a one-minute check-in during the set day will help to integrate whatever you have been emotionally working with.

Exercise 4.2 uses a pendulum to access information from the unconscious or the inner child. The more relaxed you are, the easier this exercise will be. Do not try to move the pendulum, it will move by itself. I do not know why it moves as it does, but it becomes a link from your inner child to the adult. You can use the pendulum for retrieving a vast amount of information from your unconscious, and even finding misplaced objects or interpreting dreams.

Intuitive Dialogue. Establish a rapport with your inner child. Sit on a cushion, close your eyes and imagine that your inner child is sitting in front of you.

EXERCISE 4.2: PENDULING

Time: 15-20 minutes
Setting: Where you will not be disturbed
Music: None
Lighting: Natural
Props: A pendulum (a cord, chain or string about 15-20 cm long with a heavy object on it), paper and a pen
Partner or friend: Not required

Take three deep breaths before you start. Hold the end of the cord, chain or string between your thumb and forefinger, relax your wrist and allow the pendulum to hang down. Usually it starts to move by itself within a few seconds; if this is not the case, say yes to yourself a few times and relax. Clear your mind of any thoughts and try again. Sometimes the movements are very subtle, other times they are large swings. To establish a dialogue with your inner child you need to find out what each pendulum movement means. The pendulum can move clockwise, counter-clockwise, backwards, forwards and side-to-side. You need to determine:

- the direction that means "yes"
- the direction that means "no"
- the direction that means "I don't know"
- the direction that means "I don't want to tell you"

Make your questions simple and straightforward, for example:

- Do I want to be single at the moment?
- Am I open to having fun?
- Am I willing to... ?
- Do I feel relaxed about my body?
   On a piece of paper write the direction your pendulum

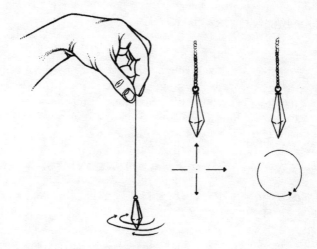

Penduling. Hold the end of the cord, string or chain between your thumb and forefinger, relax your wrist and allow the pendulum to hang down. The pendulum will move in various directions to allow you to access information from your inner child.

gives for each question. Every time you do pendulum work you will have to recheck the directions as they often change.

Ask one question at a time. When you have the answer move the pendulum up a few centimetres to stop the movement, then bring it down again to start the next question. Once you have established this form of communication with your inner child you can find out about your strategies and what motivates your behaviour. Your adult self then needs to bring the issue into the present.

Use these questions to find out how to make changes in your life. An example of dialogue you can use is below:

ADULT: Do you feel relaxed about your body?
CHILD: No.
ADULT: I know you are not feeling relaxed now, but there are times when we have felt relaxed and there is no reason we can't again.
CHILD: But my partner touched me in a way which scares me.
ADULT: I am really pleased you told me that, we need to do something about it. And I won't let this happen again.
CHILD: I feel much more relaxed now.
ADULT: Remember that I am here to protect you and I love you very much, let's have a cuddle.

You may need to do this exercise every day for some time as you work through various issues. Often, when the change we want in our life doesn't happen, we feel disappointed. The reason the change is not happening is because there is something in the way – we might want closeness and love but believe we do not deserve it. Once you realise this, it is much easier for the change to happen, and you will trust yourself to decide what you really need, rather than simply what you want right now.

Panic attacks

The number of people who suffer from panic attacks is greatly increasing and this disorder, where sufferers are rendered immobile through terror, requires careful psychological care. It is characterised by sudden overwhelming fear, so severe that those in its grip are debilitated and cannot function normally. Attacks may come just once in a lifetime or be an ongoing part of life. There are many strategies to deal with panic attacks and they require an understanding of what is happening in the body during an attack. This frequently includes over-breathing, sweating, dizziness, nausea, and a feeling of being consumed by fear.

The following technique is a variation of Exercise 4.2 using a percentage graph. This technique will help you understand what is causing your anxiety and it can also help you access a vast amount of information from your unconscious.

Place your pendulum over the centre of the percentage graph to start. Breathe deeply, closing your eyes and relaxing, bringing yourself into the present. Remind yourself of ways you can support who you are and use internal dialogue, such as "You are not alone" and "I love you", as well as hugging yourself or a cushion. The questions below are a guide only, you can deviate from them, but use the percentage graph to chart your responses.

- To what degree do you feel comfortable with your life at the moment?
- To what degree do you know that I am always here to help you?
- To what degree do you believe that when you have your next panic attack I will be there to help you?

If answers to your questions fall into the low range on the percentage graph and your desired outcome is a high range, it means that your inner child is fearful and panicky. To change this pattern and take the pendulum to a higher percentage, you will need to distance yourself from the problem.

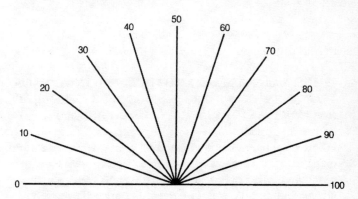

Percentage Graph. Use this and your pendulum to ask questions of your unconscious.

TIPS: DEALING WITH FEAR

Let yourself imagine the worst thing that can happen to you; really go into the fantasy of it, then ask: What are the consequences of this? What is behind this fear? What is the worst thing possible? Then imagine this happening.

It is very important that you go to the root of the fear, which will be a very familiar place because it goes back to your survival as a child.

Bring yourself back to reality by using the here and now technique and allow yourself to see that the fear is based on a four-year-old's view of the world, and not on your present situation.

Every time you feel separate from everyone around you, or worry about your survival, or use an inappropriate strategy, you create anxiety. This separates you from your inner wisdom.

Ian had been sexually abused as a child and panic and fear were an integral part of his sexual relationships. I worked with him using Exercises 4.1 and 4.2 and he was able to consciously acknowledge these traumatic experiences and create a distance for himself from his previous fearful behaviour. His commitment to working on being in the present offered him a new way to relate on an emotional and sexual level. As his communication became clearer this shifted his sexual fear.

INTERVIEW

ESME HOLMES, JUNGIAN ANALYTICAL PSYCHOTHERAPIST, TRAINED IN GROUP PROCESSING, DRUG DEPENDENCE, NARRATIVE, ART THERAPY, AND PSYCHODRAMA

When a human being is violated by sexual abuse as a child, or adult, many aspects of the self are affected – physically, psychologically, psychically, intellectually and spiritually. For healing to take place we need to work with ourselves in positive, nurturing ways. One way of doing this is to listen to our inner child, who can give us direction on how to meet our needs.

The life pattern of expressing and getting our needs met was set in childhood, but we may not have been shown how to express these needs and get them met in a positive, safe way. To meet the needs of a person who is experiencing the effects of sexual abuse, it is essential to create a safe environment. We then open ourselves to caring and listening to the true needs of the child and attempting to meet them. Sometimes this may be difficult because our adult side has internalised negative messages, particularly around the time of abuse. This can mean blaming ourselves, believing that it was our fault, holding feelings of shame and guilt, believing that we are bad or dirty and being too frightened to tell anyone.

These messages build a wall of fear around the inner child and leaves the person feeling isolated. To establish a healing relationship it is essential to connect every day with your inner child, to define its needs for the day. Creating a positive nurturing cycle will allow a loving relationship to develop with yourself and with others. Where situations of sexual abuse have not been healed, there is a risk of developing dependent ways of coping, such as drug abuse, alcoholism, gambling, eating disorders and dependent relationships.

Exercise 4.3 is designed to help you become aware of your parental conditioning. It is not about changing anything, it is about seeing the strategies you have chosen and understanding what motivates them.

EXERCISE 4.3: INNER CHILD'S RELATIONSHIP WITH PARENTS

Time: An afternoon or evening
Setting: Somewhere you will not be disturbed
Music: Optional, but must be non-intrusive
Lighting: Clear
Props: Writing pad and paper, photos of parents or caregivers
Partner or friend: Not required

Take three deep breaths and let your body relax. Imagine your mother or female caregiver, either by visualising her, from a photo, or getting a sense of how she felt. When you are ready open your eyes. List the things you have in common with your mother or caregiver, and the things about yourself which are completely different. These may be physical, emotional, intellectual, or based on your interests, values, work, taste in clothes or food, and your lifestyle When you have completed this list do the same for your father or male caregiver. If you were brought up by a single parent or in an institution do the exercise using the person who represented the primary caregiver in your life.

Once you have made this list use the pendulum and the percentage graph to ask the following questions

• To what degree are you open to looking at your relationship with your mother?
• To what degree are you open to looking at your relationship with your father?
• To what degree are you open to seeing your mother as a person?
• To what degree are you open to seeing your father as a person?
• To what degree is it threatening for you to see your mother as having normal human failings?
• To what degree is it threatening for you to see your father as having normal human failings?

Once you have pinpointed the similarities and differences, see how these behaviours have become strategies for finding or rejecting love; for example: "I find it difficult to express my feelings because I am like my father"; "My parents were never there for me, so I decided to do everything my way because I could not rely on them"; "My mother over-reacted and therefore so do I". As an adult these strategies make it very difficult to create intimacy in a relationship. By becoming consciously aware of these patterns you can use penduling to help change it.

Ask yourself the following questions to help raise your awareness:

- To what degree do I see it as important to express my feelings?
- To what degree do I realise that to have closeness and love in my life I have to be open to expressing my feelings?
- To what degree do I see that not sharing my emotions stops me from getting what I want?
- Now to what degree am I open to expressing my feelings?

The point of using the pendulum is to create more of an inner connection between the inner child and the adult which will help you get what you want out of life. By repeating the first question at the end of the sequence, you will be able to see if anything has shifted. If it has not, repeat the questions again, delving deeper into the issue.

Being at home with yourself

The more you are able to be present with your feelings and emotions, the easier it is to be relaxed with yourself. Much of the inner confusion we feel is about not being able to decipher what is still affecting us from the past, or living in a projection of what we want the future to be. These tips on being in the here and now can be used daily to help you truly be present and live in the moment, not in the past or in the future When you are healing past traumas, it is essential that you are able to bring yourself back to the here and now, using your senses to connect with what is around you.

I believe there are two ways of being in the world. You can put your energy out strongly, really feeling yourself wanting to achieve and make things happen. The alternative is to let the world come to you, opening yourself to the positive possibilities of life, which is a much more relaxed way of being. It is important to be aware which one of these two behaviours we are acting out at any time. Both are valuable ways of being, but much tension can be created if we are solely putting our energy out, trying hard to make the world work in the way we desire. We see this when we go on a holiday and it takes us a long time to unwind because we have been so strongly in action mode. Quiet, reflective time is also important. In this space we can accept the gifts which come from the universe – often, if we still our minds long enough, the answers to our problems come to us.

TIPS: BEING IN THE HERE AND NOW

Look around you and become aware of your body. Describe to yourself everything you see, feel or hear; for example, "I am sitting on the floor, feeling the cushion beneath me, my hands are resting in my lap. I can hear the noise of cars going by outside. I can see the sun shining in through the window and I can feel my breath going in and out."

Stimulate your senses by smelling the things around you and feeling with your hands; if you are in a room, feel the walls and floor; if you are outside, smell the grass or plants. Consciously hear any sounds and allow yourself to become very present in the moment.

You can ask yourself, "Who am I?" and answer, "I am the feeling in my eyes as I read this line"; "I am the movement of my hand as I turn the page"; "I am the sensation in my belly".

Be aware of your breath as you consciously breathe deeply in and out. Take three deep breaths, breathing in for a count of three and out for a count of two. Write down the two words which best describe how you are feeling right now. This helps you check your current thinking. If the two words are negative – such as "tired" and "bored" – then replace them with their opposite – "energetic" and "creative" – and see how your feelings change.

When you use this technique do not compare the positive with the negative, go into the positive only. Feel the sensations in your body when you repeat the positive words. When you finish this process, you will be peaceful and relaxed.

TIPS: FEELING GROUNDED

Feeling grounded is essential to being able to integrate the changes which have been happening in your life. I use the following simple techniques at the end of sessions or workshops. They help people cope with going back into the outside world and integrating the changes they have made or the insights they have experienced.

Close your eyes and imagine you are growing a long tail which goes down into the centre of the earth. When you arrive there, imagine a big hook onto which you tie your tail tightly.

When you are ready open your eyes, still feeling your long tail.

A variation of this exercise is to pretend you are a tree growing long roots into the earth.

Find out specifically why you enjoy being with particular people or in certain places, and what gives you pleasure in your life, by following the technique below. Either write down each question and answer, or close your eyes and do it mentally.

Choose an area you are interested in exploring on a deeper level and formulate a statement around it. You might focus on a recent happy event. For example, "I went to a party and had a really good time".

Exactly what did you enjoy?
"I met someone there I really liked."
Exactly what was it about the person that you liked?
"We talked and laughed easily and it made me feel good."
Exactly what was it about feeling good?
"When I feel good, I am very relaxed."
Exactly how does it feel when you are feeling good and relaxed?
"I feel calm and at peace, accepting what is around me and feeling contented with life."

You can also use this technique to find out exactly what you want to hear from others and reprogramme your internal tape, so that you give these messages to yourself. We all want verbal confirmation of our positive traits, but waiting for someone else to give this to us is to wait for fulfilment from another, not from yourself. This is giving your power away. So if you like other people telling you they love and appreciate you, write a list of these statements and say them to yourself on a daily basis – "I am loveable" and "I appreciate myself" are wonderful messages that you deserve to hear, but unless you really believe them it will be hard for you to accept them from anyone else.

I have used Exercise 4.4 very successfully in groups and private sessions to help people look at specific emotional behaviour they want to change. In a workshop I ran called Freeing the Wild Woman it helped many women identify what was stopping them in taking the next positive step in their lives. The exercise gave them a great insight into their emotional blocks. All of them were going through a transition: some had just had a child, some were ending a marriage, others' children had just left home, some were going through menopause.

EXERCISE 4.4: THE EXAGGERATION

Time: One to one-and-a-half hours
Setting: Anywhere you will not be disturbed
Music: Soft and relaxing
Lighting: Natural
Props: None
Partner or friend: Required

Write a list of ten things you think you cannot do in your life – these might be physical, emotional, related to your career or relationships. Start by looking at one of the outstanding ones. The statements you come up with need to be based on things you would really like to do; the statement "I cannot climb Mount Everest" is unhelpful if you have no desire to do so.

In a comfortable spot, lie down and become aware of the carpet, floor or bed beneath you. Allow yourself to sink into it with each breath. Take yourself through each part of the body allowing the ripple of relaxation to flow through the head, shoulders, neck, arms, legs and feet. Use your senses to help you relax: see your body relaxing, allow the sounds around you to take you deeper and deeper into yourself. Feel the ripple of relaxation flowing through your body as if you were being lightly massaged. With each breath experience the rise and fall of the body.

It is helpful to have someone read out the instructions below When you are ready to move on to the next point, indicate by moving a finger. Do not communicate verbally during the process as this distracts you from going deeper into the experience. If you are by yourself, make an audio tape of the instructions, starting with your first statement, and leave approximately three minutes between each point.

1. Remember the first statement you have written.
2. See yourself saying, "I can't change…"
3. Feel yourself thinking, "I don't want to change…"
4. Exaggerate this feeling of not wanting to change.
5. See what happens when you exaggerate this feeling.
6. See what you are getting out of it. What is the pay-off?
7. Now allow yourself to want to do that which you said you could not do.
8. See yourself wanting to do it.
9. Feel yourself wanting to do it.
10. Hear yourself saying, "I want to…"
11. Exaggerate this feeling of wanting to…
12. Accept this feeling and see what this does in your life.
13. Feel what it is like to do or to have or to be what you want.
14. Hear yourself say, "I have/am… in my life".

Finally have your friend or partner read both statements in the negative and positive form to you (for example, "I can't change…", negative statement; "I want to change…", positive statement) When you have finished the first change statement and have heard the negative and positive versions, continue going through each statement using the same procedure. Once you have finished allow yourself time to integrate what you have experienced. Talk it over with the person helping you, or write down your experiences in a journal or sit quietly and reflect.

Self-esteem

Self-esteem is not usually discussed when we talk about sex, so we often do not expect that a partner or friend has poor self-esteem. In my work I have heard many stories of people wanting desperately to please others and have seen the misunderstandings which then arise. A lack of positive self-esteem impacts negatively on close personal relationships, as well as on love, intimacy and sex. For self-esteem to flourish you need to resolve any underlying issues about feeling unloveable, shameful or judged by others. Feeling confident about yourself comes from a place of playfulness and an acceptance of your own style of sensual expression, which does not mimic anyone else's. Positive self-esteem will let you naturally feel good about your body's shape and how you move.

Our self-image is established by our life experiences between the ages of one and twelve. If you go back and relook at your experiences as a child you will have an understanding of how these old issues are affecting you now. The issues to look at from school are how we compared academically, at sport, in creative pursuits and with friends. At home it is our relationship with siblings and parents, and whether we received strong media messages. It is remarkable that anyone is able to develop a positive self-image. We are bombarded daily with messages that we are not quite good enough and need to change to an idealised image of beauty.

Ask yourself the following questions to test for negative self-esteem:

• When you look in the mirror do you criticise what you see?
• Do you constantly compare yourself with others?
• Do you procrastinate about getting things done, or talking to people?
• Do you shy away from challenges?
• Do you often feel you are just not good enough or smart enough?

Positive responses to any of these questions indicates that you need to work on this area.

Exercise 4.5 helps you to understand situations which trigger negative self-esteem and gives you a way to counter this. Turning the negative into the positive gives you scope to see that a situation does not have to remain as you have experienced it in the past. I have used this exercise in groups and have had a lot of success with people expanding the possibilities in their lives. It helps them move away from a negative and limited view of themselves.

EXERCISE 4.5: CHANGING NEGATIVE SELF-ESTEEM TO POSITIVE

Time: 20 minutes
Setting: Somewhere you will not be disturbed, preferably indoors
Music: Ambient or relaxing
Lighting: Soft
Props: None
Partner or friend: Not required

Start by doing Exercise 2.8. After the body is totally relaxed, take your awareness to your left hand, gently lifting it into the air and leaving the elbow on the carpet. Relax the wrist. Imagine a negative situation to do with your self-esteem and go into the experience as much as possible. When you are ready, place your hand back on the carpet. Bring your right hand up and imagine that a fairy godmother or godfather is there to grant your wish. Imagine the same situation, but as positively as you can. The more creative you can be, the better the exercise works. You can change the environment, the people involved, the situation. Imagine the best possible outcome for yourself. Put the right hand down. Gradually bring both hands up at the same time and repeat the positive right-handed fantasy once more. Repeat, bringing both hands up at the same time.

Rhonda did this exercise with me in a private session, first recalling how she reacted when she met people she did not know in a social setting. She felt shy, self-conscious and awkward, and so she avoided these situations. When she did this exercise, she could see that she actually wanted to be like her sister, who was very extroverted, and she was able to tap into a side of herself that she had not realised existed. Later she was able to see that because she had thought she did not want to be like her sister she had adopted the opposite behaviour, but this had left her socially limited. When she understood this, she was able to be consciously aware of her patterns and change and relax in the way she wanted to.

EXERCISE 4.6: CREATIVE SELF-ESTEEM

Time: 30 minutes
Setting: Somewhere you will not be disturbed
Music: None
Lighting: Soft
Props: Photos of yourself as a child; toys, games or blanket you had as a child
Partner or friend: Not required

Find a comfortable chair which has good back support and have your props near you. Allow your eyes to gently close and in your own time take three deep breaths. As you breathe out let go of the concerns of the outside world and connect with your relaxation. Let your body sink into the support around you. Just focus on your body now, letting yourself feel any tension being lightly massaged away, and move down into warmth as you let yourself go. Take time to hear any sounds outside and take yourself deeper and deeper. See how many muscles you can let go of and watch the rise and fall of each breath. Let yourself go into the comfort which is beneath you and all around you. When you are ready open your eyes.
Recall a time in your childhood when you were happily playing. It could have been at school, in a park, at a beach or at home. Use the props by your side to help you. Feeling and smelling the toys or looking at old photos of yourself as a child will help. Close your eyes and recall any image which helps you, or the feeling of a child playing. Open your eyes and talk to this child, asking how they feel. Take time to feel what the child's experience is. Put your hand over the photo of yourself, or cuddle the toy and see what it is like to be playful. Say to yourself, "I am a playful child who wants to explore this experience".

Another way you can express this creativity is by spreading shaving cream on your body and drawing shapes in the foam with your finger, or building sandcastles making collages of leaves or shells, or playing in the dirt in the garden.
The play experience allows you to be sensually creative and to be more playful with others. The experience of play is not about focusing

on a predetermined outcome, but taking time to enjoy what you are doing. Comparison is the opposite of acceptance and takes you away from being present. During this exercise many people come to the realisation that they never experienced a playful childhood. If this is true for you, now is the time to find the playfulness which was not possible when you were young. Explore this through buying yourself toys, books or games to play with, and incorporate a play-time into your life; it will help you on your journey to a strong, positive sense of self-esteem.

There are different ways to explore your inner child and Exercise 4.7 gives you help in reading your childhood messages or story, which is expressed in the picture you draw.

EXERCISE 4.7: DRAWING THE INNER CHILD

Time: 30 minutes
Setting: Somewhere you will not be disturbed
Music: Optional
Lighting: Clear
Props: Drawing pad, crayons or pencils
Partner or friend: Not required

Start by drawing pictures of yourself as a child, first with your mother and then another with your father. Do not worry about how technically good your drawing is, this exercise is not about creating an artwork but about your inner child's expression. Complete the pictures before you read on.

Take a few deep breaths and look at these pictures as if you were seeing them for the first time. Look at the subtleties in the drawings; they can help you unlock hidden emotional information about the state of your inner child and the relationship you had with your parents. Consider:

- How large or small is the child in relation to the parent?
- What is the position between the child and the adult?
- Is the child connected with the parent or separate from them?
- What is the relation of their arms and hands?
- Are the child and parent touching?
- Is the child happy, sad, angry, alone or misunderstood?
- Is the parent frustrated, angry or happy?

One of my clients drew a figure of himself as a child with no hands or arms, which symbolised his feelings of powerlessness with his father. His drawing gave him a great insight into his underlying feeling of disempowerment in his relationship with his father, which had never been resolved.

INTERVIEW

KEVIN OLVER, PSYCHOLOGIST AND CLINICAL HYPNOTHERAPIST, AND SPECIALIST IN THE FIELD OF HUMAN CONSCIOUSNESS. HE LECTURES AND TRAINS WIDELY THROUGHOUT AUSTRALIA, USA AND THE UK.

Everyone has a child inside them. We know this child when someone gives us a present, and we feel this child when someone forgets to give us a present. When we begin to really look we see that we are acting out of this inner-child space for much of our lives, and if we take the time to consciously connect with and heal this inner child we free ourselves to be who we really are and stop living life out of reactions The inner child allows us to respond to the moment and enjoy life to the fullest with a child's energy, spontaneity, playfulness and sense of wonder. When we look with the eyes of a small child we see all these qualities in the world. Look around at their adults – it is rare to see this inner light shining.

Part of the process of healing ourselves lies in reconnecting with the energy of the inner child and freeing ourselves to live joyously, not in a childish way but in a childlike way. Unless we reconnect with the inner child we remain disconnected with our vulnerability and sensitivity. On my own journey I have looked closely at who I thought I was, who I was trying to be, and the image of myself I was trying to present to the world. I have also had to look at who I was trying just as hard not to be, and who I was trying to hide from the world. When I came to experience both, and see them for what they were, I was able to bring my awareness to these dual conflicting energies.

5

Mates in Heaven: Intimacy for Couples

It is very difficult to create a feeling of intimacy with another person if you do not feel relaxed and connected to yourself. A healthy relationship with yourself must come first, before any successful relationship with someone else is possible. If you are having trouble establishing a positive relationship with your partner, this chapter will give you practical exercises, tips and strategies to help you both. When we have sex we are seeking a meaningful connection with another, but unless an emotional rapport has been established prior to the sex we can be left feeling hurt, disappointed and rejected. This feeling can also occur in long-term relationships when couples have lost touch with one another.

I often get women coming into the shop who would like their partner, whether male or female, to change. They want them to become more communicative, attentive, affectionate, assertive in bed, or to put the same amount of energy into the relationship as they do in order to improve their sex life. But the bottom line is that you cannot make someone do something they do not want to do. If your partner does not have the same priorities around your relationship as you do, you will only create more tension and frustration if you try to change them. This is why the emphasis in this book is on you being happy and fulfilled in yourself: out of this place of relaxation a new style of relating can develop where you can work on the issues together.

May, an attractive woman in her forties, was distressed because her husband had recently confessed to having had a long-term affair with another woman, and they had a child together. She was angry and resentful, and she wanted to purchase a product that would solve her problem. I knew there was no sex toy or book which could bring them back together in a loving way, yet she perused the shelves intensely looking for a solution to her problem. I tried to explain my approach to sexual healing, stressing the need to fulfil and love yourself first before you are able to have a good relationship with another, but to no avail. Customers were purchasing vibrators, dildos and other sexual products. May asked me how the sex toys could be used. She started to relax, and decided to purchase a vibrator and a sex education video. I was pleased to see her a couple of days later with a big smile on her face. She told me, "I feel so much happier, I am really enjoying the toy I bought. I don't care what my husband does anymore, the main thing is that I feel good." She had realised that her sexual fulfilment was important, and from a place of loving and valuing herself she could make decisions about what she wished to do in her marriage.

Many couples who come to me for counselling cannot express their love for each another. When I ask them what positive relationship role models they have had in their life they look at me blankly. They tell me that their parents did not have a good relationship, or that their mother always felt a certain amount of resentment towards their father. I have often heard my clients say that they did not ever see their parents touch or spend time together. In short, they had no experience of seeing a good relationship and therefore found it difficult to create a healthy,; loving connection of their own.

Martha and William were in their mid-thirties and had been referred to me by their counsellor because they had not had sex for three years. They had been married for seven years and had two small children. William worked long hours in a high-pressure job and Martha studied part-time, as well as looking after the household and children. Their courtship had been short and initially they said their sex life had been "all right", but since the birth of their first child they had only made love very occasionally. I saw them individually at first and then later in a joint session.

I took William through Exercises 2.3-2.7 and he told me that he felt out of touch with his body, overweight, but not able to exercise because of his bad back. Our first session together brought up a lot of his frustration. When I saw Martha, she also complained of being overweight, but she had recently started exercising and said she was now feeling better about her body. In their joint session they discussed what prevented them spending time together and Martha complained there was no affection between them.

I advised them to do Exercise 5.1, which worked wonderfully, allowing them the space and time to reconnect with one another and leading to an evening of erotic passion. William said that this exercise helped him feel loved, which allowed him to be open to his body and to Martha's needs. Martha heard what she had longed for – that she was loved and appreciated. To break the negative patterns they had established in their relationship they made a commitment to spending quality time together each week, and to complimenting each other on a daily basis and expressing affection regularly. They also put time aside to touch each other lovingly and nurture their new connection. If you have not felt close to your partner for some time the exercise below will give you a wonderful way to re-establish an emotional rapport. It will also enable already close couples to go deeper into their intimacy.

EXERCISE 5.1: LOVE AND APPRECIATION

Time: 40-60 minutes
Setting: A room where you will not be disturbed
Music: Soft, sensuous, but not intrusive
Lighting: Dimmed, or candlelight
Props: Two large cushions
Partner or friend: Partner required

Sit against a wall, making yourself comfortable on a cushion, with your legs out straight in front of you. Your partner should sit between your legs, letting their head rest on your shoulder. Move the cushions around to make yourselves as comfortable as possible. Place one hand on your genitals or belly, and the other hand over your partner's heart. Close your eyes and take three deep breaths together, feeling the body gently rise and fall. Start by saying all the things you love and appreciate about your partner. Draw on a special time or a particular quality which has touched you. The partner receiving this acknowledgment should not talk, just accept what is being said. If there are moments of silence do not worry, just sit quietly and let yourselves be close together. When you are ready, swap over. After the exercise hold one another and take time to connect in a gentle, loving way.

Communication, forgiveness and trust

The secret to a successful, long-term, happy relationship is friendship, forgiveness, trust and communication. We have to learn these things as we go along. Having a good relationship means accepting that it is a process of trial and error, but these three ingredients are essential. If we do not have honest communication we cannot feel emotionally connected to our partner, and it will be very difficult to feel loving and sexual towards them. Discovering your partner's needs, anxieties and desires, as well as sharing your own, will lead to a deeper understanding and a depth of emotional intimacy. Finding a common, comfortable vocabulary to share, which can include clear, non-verbal signs, will help you relate in a more positive way. For some people, discussing sex in a non-sexual situation is less stressful. By being honest in your communication you will take your relationship to a new level of emotional intimacy.

Love and appreciation. Allow you and your partner to reconnect with one another before an evening of erotic passion.

TIPS: IMPROVED COMMUNICATION

Start by writing down a list of topics you both wish to discuss.

Set up a time when you will not be disturbed and sit opposite one another. Both of you should close your eyes and connect with yourself first. Then take three deep breaths.

Do not concentrate on what you want to say, but how your body is feeling. Does it feel tight or relaxed) If it is tight, where in your body are you holding tension) Breathing deeply into this area will help you relax.

Become aware of your expectations and be open to listening to your partner. Allow silence to be part of your conversation – this can be a way of new information coming to the surface.

Take turns to speak, and as you listen do not have an internal dialogue going on with prepared answers.

Become aware of your voice and the tone you are using to express yourself. Do you sound angry or condescending?

Notice how you use your eyes. Do you look at your partner when you are communicating?

Be aware of your body language. Are your arms crossed in front of you? The more relaxed you are in your posture, the more open you will be in communicating.

Our needs in a relationship are often pushed aside, ultimately causing a great deal of tension. When couples do not put time aside to regularly discuss what they want out of their relationship, resentment builds up. If you do Exercise 5.2 regularly, it will help you to be clear to your self and your partner about your relationship expectations. When you only express your needs to your partner in a time of crisis it places great stress on the connection between you.

EXERCISE 5.2: WHAT DO I NEED?

Time: One hour
Setting: In a natural setting, park, beach
Music: None
Lighting: Optional
Props: None
Partner or friend: Partner required

Both of you should write a list of your needs, and taking time to reflect on what has been happening to you lately. Sit in a quiet place facing one another, close your eyes and take three deep breaths. Take it in turns to express the needs that you have written down. When it is your turn to listen, do not interrupt and when your partner has finished sit in silence, taking in what you have heard before replying. Sharing in this way will strengthen your communication. You may need to set time aside the following day to reflect on any issues which have arisen.

Forgiveness is the act of healing yourself of the anger, resentment and hurt you feel towards your partner, and recognising and experiencing the pain you are holding in your body. To forgive is not about forcing yourself to forget and let go. It is initially just about exploring your emotions, dealing with the problem by yourself, and then coming back to your partner to discuss the issue which has arisen in your relationship. If you are not able to forgive your partner for what they have done, it will be very difficult for you to recreate a feeling of love and intimacy between you.

EXERCISE 5.3: FORGIVENESS – INDIVIDUAL CONNECTION

Time: 45-60 minutes
Setting: Somewhere private where you can scream and shout without being disturbed
Music: Initially relaxing and soothing, then rhythmical, African, or drum music
Lighting: Natural or soft
Props: Two cushions
Partner or friend: Not required

Start by using Exercise 3.4 to locate any tension in your body. Expand this awareness to include any thoughts or feelings you have which are associated with the issue of forgiveness. When you are ready, open your eyes and sit on a cushion, placing the other cushion in front of you. Let the cushion symbolise your partner and express any frustration, shame or rage by talking or yelling at it. Spend 15-20 minutes saying what is on your mind, no matter how irrational, abusive or unreasonable.

Put on rhythmical, African or drum music and shake, jump and a scream, moving your body in time with the music. Punch the cushion, and for 15-20 minutes express what is happening for you, until you are physically exhausted. Turn the music off and sit or lie still, quietly connecting with yourself and what is happening in your body. If you need to, go back and do Exercise 3.4 once more.

The second forgiveness exercise is done with your partner. I first did this in a workshop where we had to learn to relate without words. It is a very powerful way to connect with a partner, because it enables you to go deeper into the love between you. As I have discussed earlier, there are two ways of connecting to the universal power – one is to actively go out and create what you want in your life, and the other is to allow life to come to you. This exercise is about expanding your receptivity.

EXERCISE 5.4: FORGIVENESS – COUPLES CONNECTING

Time: 30 minutes
Setting: Somewhere private
Music: Relaxing and soothing
Lighting: Soft lighting or candles
Props: Two cushions
Partner or friend: Partner required

Sit on cushions opposite one another, both placing your right hand on the middle of your partner's chest. You should place your left hand over your partner's right hand and close your eyes, taking a few deep breaths together and centring yourselves. In your own time open your eyes and look into your partner's. Connect to your partner from a soft loving space, without judgement. You might find this initially a bit embarrassing, or that you laugh – this is fine. Take the time to sit and just be with whatever you experience and allow your partner's gaze to come to you. From this place of connection take turns to express the hurt and emotional pain you both have felt. Allow all emotions out and do not censor. Finish with Exercise 5.1.

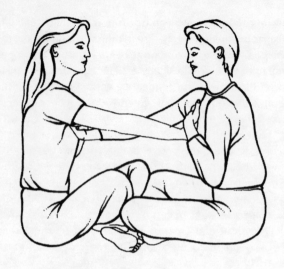

Forgiveness. Connect with your partner and go deeper into the love between you.

INTERVIEW

ELISABETH SHAW, REGIONAL MANAGER AND CLINICAL CONSULTANT, RELATIONSHIPS AUSTRALIA (NSW)

When couples work on intimacy and sexuality they are asking each other to be vulnerable within the relationship. This can be a hard thing to do because so much of our self-esteem and validation comes from what our partner thinks of us. To ask our partner to step outside their comfort zone and do something different, especially around sexuality, often creates fear because it raises the potential of being exposed, or even shamed, in front of someone whose opinion they care about. Many people come to see me wanting to learn tools to heal and change their relationship, but they are unwilling to do this if it means vulnerability or embarrassment. People must be willing to move outside their comfort zones to address their problems of intimacy and sexuality. Rather than deal with these issues, many people will subsume their frustration with their relationship in an affair, a one-night stand or a visit to a sex worker. Sex with a stranger is emotionally safe because there is nothing invested in this transitory relationship.

Many couples find it difficult to heal intimacy and trust issues on their own, and that is where a trained professional can help, giving them ways to get through blocks in their relationship and allowing change to occur. Often, as couples diminish their anxiety around intimacy and sexuality, they move the shame and vulnerability to another place. Individual therapy, as well as couples counselling, can be helpful to assist each partner to address their own emotional blocks. People often fear their partner's reaction to the issues they raise, but I have found that once problems are aired there is a great sense of relief for both partners. A good couples therapist relates sexual issues to their emotional base, because it is important to realise that this is where the problem lies, not just in the sexual behaviour itself.

Trust in a relationship includes clear, relaxed communication and being able to give and receive freely. When I first did Exercise 5.5 I had a great insight into the way I attempted to control people and situations, and saw many of my long-standing emotional patterns. A couple I know do this exercise on special occasions, including birthdays.

EXERCISE 5.5: DEVELOPING TRUST

Time: Two to two-and-a-half hours
Setting: Any environment
Music: Optional
Lighting: Optional
Props: Optional
Partner or friend: Partner required

Decide who will be Partner A or B for the first hour. Partner B can only reply yes to anything they are asked to do. For Partner A, this part of the exercise is about receiving as Partner B gives. This exercise is not about creating tension, anger or resentment between the two of you.

Examine what you would like your partner to emotionally and physically give to you. Perhaps you can create an experience that enables you to go deeper into the love and acceptance of each other, for example, receiving a massage or having a meal cooked for you. After one hour discuss your experiences then swap. The first time you do this exercise you may like to include some boundaries before you both start. As you become more familiar with this exercise you can increase the time you spend on it from a few hours to a whole day.

Part of trust and friendship in a relationship is knowing why you react the way you do. This next exercise will give you an unusual insight into how your mind works and reveal childhood patterns which might still be affecting you. It helps you to see what happens when you are taken on a visual exploration. Through it you can gain great insight into how your mind evaluates experiences, and the way you think and react. You may be able to see why you have particular thoughts about the things you are shown. As your partner guides you, it can bring up issues of trust and this can expand your communication. It might stimulate your sense of colour, light and texture. I have noticed that when I do this exercise colours seem brighter and I take life less for granted. Sensory deprivation often leads us to appreciate things on a deeper level.

EXERCISE 5.6: THE CAMERA

Time: One hour
Setting: Inside or outside
Music: None
Lighting: Natural
Props: Whatever you have at hand, or specially chosen objects
Partner or friend: Partner required

Decide who will he Partner A and who will be Partner B. Partner A closes their eyes and the only time they open them is when Partner B says "click". There is to be no conversation during this exercise. Using clear communication, Partner B guides Partner A around the environment you have chosen; for example, "There is one step in front of you" or "Turn to the left. The point of the exercise is for Partner B to take care of

Partner A and to he as creative as possible with the items placed in front of Partner A's eyes.

Partner B says "click", and Partner A quickly opens and closes their eyes, just long enough to see the image in front of them. This might be a photo, a rock, part of Partner B's body, food, or some household object.

After twenty minutes, discuss the experience and swap over.

Creating emotional and physical intimacy

An essential component to a good relationship is a very simple one: appreciating the person in your life. Often our lives are so hectic that we forget how important our partner is to us. If you remember to say something every day to make your partner feel loved and appreciated it will make a remarkable difference to the dynamic between you. Such expressions make your partner feel valued, and they can be as simple as "I am so glad you are in my life"; "I really appreciate the fact that you did the shopping for me today"; "You look wonderful in that outfit"; "I love us doing things together" or "I think you are sexy". All these positive loving statements lay a foundation for intimacy. Initially you may find this difficult, but after a short time it will become easier for you to focus on the positive elements in your partner and to express them. Leaving a loving message on a notepad or the answering machine takes only a minute and yet it will make your partner feel special for hours.

Every relationship needs a commitment to quality time, if not daily then no less than weekly. Put time aside to do things together; otherwise, as the relationship grows and develops, it will be difficult to stay connected. You may spend time together as simply as going for a walk, during which time you catch up on what has been happening in your life, or taking up a sporting or recreational interest together. It is important that the time you spend with each other is on something you both enjoy, so that you can make it special.

I have used Exercise 5.7 with people who have had great difficulty feeling connected to their partner. Only by looking at the issues which are stopping you connecting can you clear them away.

EXERCISE 5.7: CREATING INTIMACY

Time: 30 minutes
Setting: A room where you will not be disturbed
Music: None
Lighting: Natural
Props: None
Partner or friend: Partner required

Begin this exercise alone, closing your eyes, taking three deep breaths and asking yourself, "How am I feeling at the moment? Do I feel open to being closer to my partner?" If the answer is no, speak to your inner child, reminding yourself how important It is to have love and closeness in your life. Remind yourself of the things you have enjoyed with your partner in the past, and tell yourself that you are now ready for your next emotional step. Ask again whether you are open to being closer to your partner.

If the answer is still no, do Exercises 2.3, 2.4, 2.6 and 2.7, which will allow you to release some of the tension in your body. Finish with a visualisation of being emotionally and physically close to your partner. Include how it feels to be loved and nurture and see your boundaries expanding.

This next part of the exercise you do with your partner. Sit opposite one another, both closing your eyes and taking three belly breaths. When you feel open to talking to your partner, ask the how they are feeling. Tell them how you would like to be close t them and what you would like to do with them. Even if you have prearranged what you will be doing it is important to check in with your partner to reconfirm that they still feel the same. If you are feeling apprehensive, express this – remember that you are expanding your boundaries and intimacy. For some people this is frightening, but let this fear be mixed with the excitement that you are taking a wonderful step forward in your relationship.

EXERCISE 5.8: WORDS AND MUSIC OF LOVE

Time: 20-30 minutes
Setting: Somewhere you will not be disturbed

Music: Optional, if you chose music make it ambient, string or woodwind instruments
Lighting: Soft or candlelight
Props: A photo of your partner, or an object which reminds you of them, writing paper and pen
Partner or friend: Not required

This exercise is designed to inspire your artistic side, give your lover a treat, and bring some romance back into your relationship.

Sit in a comfortable position, close your eyes and take three deep belly breaths. Find your own natural rhythm and take your awareness to the space in the middle of the chest called the heart centre. As you breathe into this area, visualise your loved one and the aspects you appreciate about them. It could be the way they move, speak, laugh, hold you, or the expressions they use. Draw on these for inspiration, allowing words to come to you.

When you are ready, open your eyes and write down the words that express your feelings. Record how your partner shares these aspects of themselves with you. These words can either be set to verse, rhyme or music.

Erotic genital massage

We often base our lovemaking foreplay on our past sexual experiences. We are expected to dazzle our present lover with all the sexual tricks and erotic magic we have previously learned. The reality is that we often feel unsure and insecure in this area, not knowing what will turn ourselves and a partner on. But if you both experiment with erotic genital massage you will soon find out.

When I first did such a massage course in San Francisco, it revolutionised my ideas about erotic touch. I experienced such depths of pleasure and ecstasy during the massage that there was no turning back. In my work with couples, erotic genital massage has become an invaluable tool for increasing sexual pleasure between them and the feedback has always been overwhelmingly positive.

These massages for women and men were developed by Annie Sprinkle, with Joseph Kramer, and have been taught throughout the world. Joseph Kramer has done a lot of work with men to keep sexuality alive in situations of HIV/AIDS. This massage is an alternative to traditional sex and its essential component is the breath. The person being massaged needs to place more emphasis on the inhale than the exhale, and allow the breath to form a regular rhythm, as the more you breathe, the more pleasure you will feel. The person massaging also needs to be aware of their own breath and to encourage their partner to breathe deeply. The purpose of the massage is to pulse sexual energy from the genitals throughout the body, and this is done through conscious breathing.

This massage will give your partner the opportunity to take their bodily pleasure to new heights. Clear communication is essential. Your partner needs to tell you if they would like a lighter or heavier touch, or less of one stroke and more of another. Any of these techniques can be included in lovemaking. This massage can also bring up a lot of pain and trauma from the past, as many people realise they have never been touched in the manner they have wanted, or have been touched non-consentingly. If this is the case, be very gentle. Often just holding your partner and letting them cry will help heal the emotional pain they are feeling. In women the G-spot is often the point where sexual trauma is lodged. This massage has been developed to allow couples to go deeper into their sexual pleasure; if appropriate wear latex gloves and use a condom over the vibrator.

EXERCISE 5.9: ECSTATIC EROTIC GENITAL MASSAGE FOR WOMEN

Time: One to one-and-a-half hours
Setting: Somewhere private
Music: For the first 45 minutes, music with a rhythmical and relaxing beat, such as k.d. Lang, Gloria Estefan, Marvin Gaye, Govi, Celine Dion. After the massage, ambient music – your favourite classical track or recordings of the sounds of nature.
Lighting: Soft, clear light
Props: Massage table or bed (if none available this can be done on the floor), sheet, towel, cushions, massage oil, water-based lubricant, candles, a plug-in massager or vibrator
Partner: Partner required
Note: Short fingernails are necessary for the internal massage, or you can use latex surgical gloves

Warm the massage oil by placing the bottle in hot water for five to ten minutes. Put a large sheet on your massage surface with a towel over it. Your partner needs to be naked, lying comfortably; on her stomach, with her arms and legs uncrossed by her sides. It is important that the partner giving the massage is very relaxed: if you are standing, bend your knees; if you are kneeling or sitting, make sure you are comfortable. You will need to be naked for the body slide, so if you are wearing clothing make sure it can be easily discarded, or do the massage naked.

Start by gently rubbing your partner's scalp with the tips of your fingers. Do this for a few minutes, then place one hand in between your partner's shoulder blades and the other on the lower back, and together take three deep breaths. As you both inhale push the belly out as much as you can, and on the exhale just let go. Run the warmed massage oil over the back of your hands and let it drip onto the body. Move the palms of your hands along the curves of her body and keep breathing with your partner. At every stage of the massage check in with her and see how she is feeling about what you are doing. This part of the massage takes about ten minutes. Next, use your body to gently slide along your partner's back until your face is against the back of her head and your bodies are completely touching. Run your hands from the back of her shoulders along the length of her arms, and put the palms of your hands over the back of her hands, interlacing your fingers. Whisper words of love and caring in her ear – "I love the feel of your body"; "Your skin feels so soft" or "You are so sexy". Your feet can be used to massage her calves, ankles and feet. Imagine you are a sexy snake working your magic up the body. When you have had fun with the body slide, turn your lover over.

Place your fingers either side of each of her fingernails and press the side of her fingers deeply, then do the same with the toes. This stimulates the points where energy is released. Because of the intensity of the massage fear can often develop and signs of this are heaviness in the hands, arms, legs and feet. A massage of the fingers and toes will help. If your partner is putting more emphasis on their exhale rather than their inhale, they can develop a tingling pain in the mouth, feet and hands. Allow them to relax their breathing and to re-establish a pattern with more emphasis on the inhale than the exhale.

So, before you commence the erotic part of the exercise you should:

• do a slow massage of your partner's scalp;
• using massage oil, glide the palms of your hands all over your partner's body;
• flow into a front body slide, using slow, sensuous movement;
• massage the fingers and toes.

Rub your hands vigorously together until they are warm and place them over the ovaries (the inside of the hip bones facing the pubic hair). Gently circle the palms clockwise over the

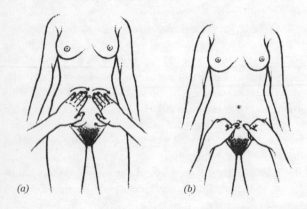

(a)   (b)

(a) Place your hands over your partner's ovaries and circle them clockwise. (b) Stimulate her external G-spot

ovaries and uterus.

Stimulate the external G-spot by placing your fingers approximately 8 cm above the pubic bone, towards the belly button.

Next rest one hand on the genitals and the other in between the breasts. Move your hands between these two points, massaging as you go.

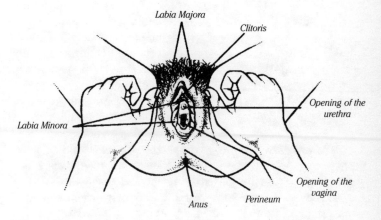

Put your thumbs at the top of the inner thigh and press inward towards the labia

Put your two thumbs at the top of the inner thigh, at the point where it joins the labia, and press along this line from the front of the body to the back, pressing inward towards the

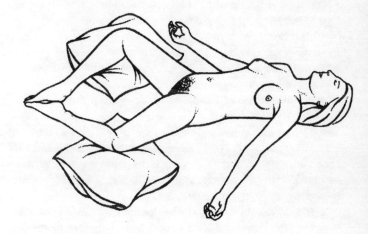

Your partner should lie flat on her back, with cushions underneath her knees, feet together and knees apart

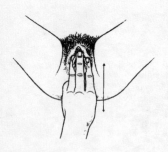

Do the 'pussy pet'.

labia.

Gently tug tufts of pubic hair. Massage the nipples, alternating between the fingertips and finger pads in a circular motion.

Now ask your partner to lie flat on her back, with cushions underneath her knees, feet together and knees apart. Cover your fingertips with water-based lubricant and move the middle three fingers up the vulva, using the longest finger to gently part the lips. Do the "pussy pet", using long, slow strokes and imagining you are petting a cat. Move along the outer labia from top to bottom and up again, including the vagina and clitoris.

With your palm over the vulva, vibrate the area. Lovingly massage the outer and inner labia between your thumb and first finger. Gently run your finger between the outer and inner labia from the perineum to above the clitoris. Using the outer edges of your hands push the outer and inner labia together. Gently tap the inner thighs and vulva with your fingers, as if playing a drum. With plenty of lubricant, massage the clitoris by gently pinching and pulling it, then use your forefinger to make little circles around it. While you are discovering the vulva with one hand you can touch your partner's breast or nipples with the other hand, in any way your partner enjoys.

Next, give your partner an internal massage. Do not allow any oil into the vaginal area because it can cause infection. Using the "pussy pet" technique, open the labia and insert one finger into the vagina. Place your other hand on the abdomen or between the breasts. Allow your finger to rest inside her, then moving it gently ask if she would like another finger inserted. Move the fingers inside her up, down and to each side. Feel the G-spot, which has a ribbed texture, on the upper wall of the vagina. When she is aroused this becomes more sensitive.

Taking your mouth to her vulva, blow warm air onto her

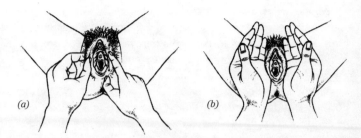

(a) Massage the inner and outer labia between your thumb and first finger. (b) Using outer edges of your hand, push the outer and inner labia together

clitoris. Use your tongue to stimulate the clitoris by sucking and running the tongue in a circular motion over it. At the same time, move your fingers in and out in a twisting motion, or stimulate the G-spot by doing a press/release movement, as though you were ringing a doorbell. Many women like manual thumb stimulation of the clitoris, alternating with oral clitoral stimulation.

Invite your partner to do kegels, clenching and relaxing the genital muscles. It is fantastic! Explore the cervix using the tips of your fingers. Some women love to have their cervix stimulated, but for others this is not comfortable, so check first. If she is bleeding be very gentle.

If she now wants deep penetration, insert more fingers as she relaxes. If your partner would like you to put your whole hand inside her, make sure she is very relaxed and breathing deeply. This must be done very slowly, almost like a meditation. Do not force your hand into her. Try putting the other hand under her tailbone, or massaging her abdomen.

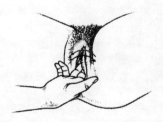

Move your fingers in and out of the vagina in a twisting motion.

Now, with the body massager or vibrator,

stimulate the bottom of her feet and then move up the body. Put the vibrator against her inner thighs and labia to allow her to become accustomed to the sensations.

Use the vibrator on the vaginal opening, then glide the vibrator around the clitoris, circling as you go. Some women do not like the vibrator placed directly on their clitoris, but to one side. On the clitoral area use a press/release movement. Expect the sexual energy to be heightened by the massager or vibrator. Orgasm is encouraged!

Some women like the sensation of external anal massage. You can do this with your fingers or a vibrator, but make sure you move from the vagina down to the anus. Do not move from the anus to the vagina, as this can transfer bacteria and cause vaginal infections.

You can finish the massage here by wrapping her in a towel and letting her relax, or she can go on to the energy orgasm, Exercise 2.7. The sexual energy created by the massage can be pulsed through the whole body by doing this exercise. Stay present, do not talk or touch her, just allow her to relax in this space. This massage can be a very intense experience and it is important to leave time to enjoy it and process any emotional issues which come up. The body will often have a tingling sensation – this is quite normal. After ten to fifteen minutes bring her a glass of water and check how she is feeling.

Jessica and her partner came to me to learn erotic massage as part of her journey of healing. As a child she had suffered many years of sexual abuse from her father and the massage gave her an understanding of the blockages she had in her body. She realised that they were areas she had repressed. The trust she had in her partner was essential, knowing that she could relax if this past trauma was released. She told me, "It was okay to cry, to be angry as well as to feel joy. It allowed me to heal because I wasn't expected to be a certain way. The vibrator was a wonderful healing tool, enabling me to go deeper into my body. Now I have learned to use these techniques by myself, as well as with my partner, and have a whole new way of relating sexually."

As a child Jo had also been sexually abused by her father, and she had worked on her sexual healing for a long time. She told me, "The real learning curve started when I did a workshop which involved nakedness, helping me to relax with my body, as I had always felt ashamed of it. I found the workshops with women invaluable as here I learned about my body and emotions. I then started to become aware of the difference between love, sex and intimacy, how they are all closely related and yet different. I had always believed that sex equalled love – this came from my background of abuse. I felt love was unachievable and sex was dirty. I was very confused about these two areas, and intimacy was never a consideration because it was not part of the love and sex I received as a child. By doing the erotic massage techniques with my partner, I could ask for what I wanted, which I had never done before, I had never had a voice. My father always asked, demanded and insisted on what he wanted, so I felt that if I asked for anything I would be as bad as he was.

"Based on this I became a much better giver. I had to learn the language to ask for what I wanted, and have the experience in order to know what I found pleasurable or not. For example, I never liked my nipples being played with very much because they are sensitive, but in the past I never had the courage to say anything. Now that has changed. I never knew I had any feeling in my body other than in my clitoris, whereas now I am aware of so many areas I like being played with. Making noise was one of my biggest changes. What was happening for me as a child was secret and I had to be silent and prevent orgasm. Now I make a point of making as much noise as I want, whenever I want to in lovemaking, making it more enjoyable.

"My greatest achievement has been learning to satisfy myself sexually. I feel confident with my partner, so that if I don't achieve an orgasm I can use a vibrator to satisfy myself. In the past this would have been taboo, as I was brought up to believe self-pleasuring was selfish. It has also allowed our relationship to go to a deeper level. Because our communication skills have developed, we can try different things and, through this, sex and erotic play have become normalised. I know sex does not have to end with sexual intercourse."

Rose and Mary, a lesbian couple who have been together for fifteen years, have lovingly incorporated the erotic massage into their life. "We put aside a whole evening and set up a sacred space to do the massage. We start with a sensual massage then move into erotic play. What has changed for us is taking more time; we awaken the skin and then go into the experience of giving and receiving, tantalising every part of our being. This creates a wonderful atmosphere to move into lovemaking or meditation, and to deepen the connection we have."

EXERCISE 5.1O: ECSTATIC EROTIC GENITAL MASSAGE FOR MEN

The requirements for this exercise are the same as for Exercise 5.9. Begin the massage in exactly the same way and continue until you have finished the finger massage.

Next, wake up the genital area by gently scratching and pulling the pubic hair and kneading the pubic mound between the fingers and thumb. (Massage oil is not required for this part of the exercise.) Stretch the scrotal skin and tickle it. Hold the tip of the penis firmly; with your other hand use your thumb and forefinger to move up the shaft, pressing deeply. Rotate your hand and work down, squeezing and kneading. Ask your partner if the pressure is strong enough. Holding the head of the penis continue to move up and down the shaft pressing deeply.

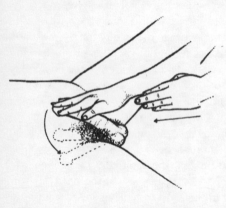

Massage your partner's penis in a circular motion.

Placing your hand on your partner's genitals, run the oil over the back of your hand and let it drip through your fingers. During this part of the massage your partner may get an erection – whether they do or not is not important. The main point is for them to experience bodily pleasure without ejaculation. Massage the penis in a continuous circular motion with your hands going in opposite directions, one pulling the skin back and the other sliding out from the base to the head of the penis. This stroke can be done with a flat hand or by wrapping the hand around the shaft. Some men like it with both hands going in the same direction. Many men find they like the penis pulled down between their legs for this.

Place the thumb and forefinger of one hand firmly at the

base of the penis, with your palm resting on the body. Turn your other hand so that it is palm up and resting on top of the first hand. Move your thumb and forefinger up the shaft of the penis, wrapping, squeezing, twisting and pulling. Use plenty of oil. Many men prefer a slow, deep stroke. When you get to the top of the penis squeeze just below the head, as if taking the

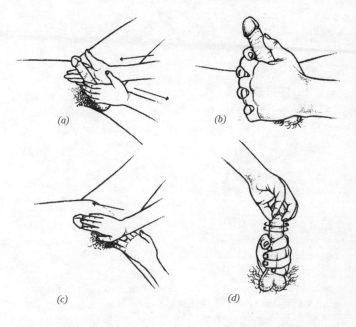

(a) Rub the penis between the palms of your hands. Imagine you are rubbing a firestick.
(b) Interlace your fingers and massage deeply. (c) Apply pressure to the penis and rub back and forth, as if ironing. (d) Do a circular motion on the head, as if juicing an orange

top off a bottle, playing with the penis as you finish the stroke.

Placing the penis between the palms of your hands, rub it backwards and forwards with a fast or slow rhythm, using medium to deep pressure. Imagine you are rubbing a firestick to create a flame. Holding the penis in this firestick position, interlace your fingers and massage deeply, using the thumbs to play with the head of the penis. You can also hold your hands still and if he is moderately erect he can move between your hands. If the penis is not erect, lay it flat against the body with

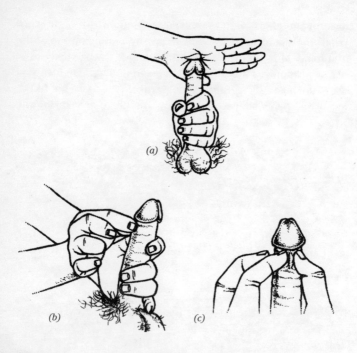

(a) Pull back the skin and rotate your palm over the eye of the penis. (b) and (c) Pinch below the head of the penis, on the side facing the body.

the head facing the belly button. Part your two middle fingers, making a V and place them either side of the base of the penis, palm up. Put your other hand over the top of your first hand, applying pressure to the penis, and rub back and forth, as if ironing it.

For the next stage, wrap your whole hand around the penis, but leave the head exposed. With the fingertips of your other hand do a circular motion on the head of the penis, as if you were juicing an orange. Use your fingernails to softly scratch behind the coronal ridge, the back of the head of the penis. Then pull back the skin from the head of the penis and with your palm outstretched gently rotate it over the eye of the penis, varying the pressure and speed.

Nestle the penis against your interlaced fingers and pinch the sensitive place below the head of the penis on the side facing the body. Use your thumbs in a circular motion to massage deeply. Vary this stroke by moving your thumbs in opposite directions with a rapid deep pressure, as if you were cross-country skiing. With your thumb and forefinger form a ring around the scrotum and the base of the penis. Pull the skin taut across the scrotum and then alternate between your fingertips and fingernails to gently stimulate this area. The scrotum is often very sensitive, so check in with your partner on how he is feeling.

Moving from the genitals up to the nipples in a circular motion, stimulate the nipples, alternating between fingertips and fingernails. It is important when massaging men to distribute the sexual energy from the genitals down to the thighs and up to the nipples and chest. You can use your forearm to move up the body from the genitals and down again, and from the inner thighs down to the knee in order to spread the energy. Alternating the pressure and stroke gives variety and stimulation and helps to pulse the sexual energy throughout the body. Another option to distribute sexual energy is to use the plug-in massager or vibrator along the shaft of the penis, under the testicles and all over the body.

If your partner feels that he is about to ejaculate, slow down your strokes and allow him to become conscious of breathing deeply into the belly. For some men, doing the energy orgasm, Exercise 2.7, a few times during the massage can be beneficial in pulsing the energy through the body. Stand back and allow him to do this without touching him.

If you are going to move into lovemaking be conscious of watching your partner's face, looking for their level of tension and relaxation. Remove all oil from the penis by rubbing down the area with a warm, wet towel. Most condoms and oil are not compatible and oil in the vagina is an irritant. At this point oral sex can be an added bonus; sucking the shaft of the penis as you massage the testicles, or using some of the pressure-point strokes can be very enjoyable.

David came to see me with his wife, to whom he had been married for ten years. They learned the ecstatic erotic genital massage and he was thrilled about how it improved their relationship. It changed his ideas about sexual touch: "I now touch with a sense of purpose, knowing what I am doing, and this has created a new depth of intimacy between us. We have gone from having a relationship which was becoming mundane to one with a new sense of adventure. I found the energy orgasm to be an amazing physical release and I cried and sobbed, letting go of emotional pain I had carried with me throughout my life. I didn't know what this pain related to, but I allowed myself to release it anyway. I now have a different approach to my wife's body and my own."

Ken and Julia have been together for nearly a decade and five years ago they came to do a massage workshop. Julia told me, "When we were first together our relationship was very experimental, and after learning the erotic sensual touch techniques from the workshop we spent time incorporating them into our lovemaking. Now we rarely have "traditional sex", because we prefer to spend our time experimenting and playing. We both have come to realise that it is not our responsibility to satisfy one another, that each of us must ask for what we want and be open to receiving it. This has allowed us to relax and enjoy with no expectations." The workshop gave Ken the ability to feel his body in a new way. "I have used the techniques to ejaculate only occasionally, but my whole body has become incredibly sensitive and my nipples and skin have become erotic zones. I love being stroked and touched, it is as pleasurable to me as an orgasm. Fantasy used to be my prime sexual motivation and I fantasised during lovemaking with my partner and during the day. After experiencing the erotic massage I found that I stopped fantasising so much and I now go into a meditative space of my own. Here everything is intensified and my awareness of touch, smell and taste is heightened."

These massage techniques cannot only spice up your sex life, they can also help when traditional sex is not possible. Heather and Ron came to see me after Ron was diagnosed with prostate cancer. He was soon to enter hospital to have the cancer removed and had been warned by his doctor that he would be unable to have an erection after the operation. They came to learn the erotic massage techniques in order to be able to continue to be sexually close to one another.

Exercise 5.11 can flow on from the erotic genital massage (for more information see Chapter 6). Many people feel very vulnerable around anal play, so you will need to discuss any reservations you might have beforehand. Clear communication is essential, especially if something does not feel pleasurable. The anus has a wealth of nerve endings, so this massage can be sensual and erotic, as well as being very relaxing and a foreplay to anal sex. As with the erotic massage, the breath is an integral component – remember to place more emphasis on the inhale than the exhale.

EXERCISE 5.11: EXTERNAL ANAL MASSAGE

Time: One hour
Setting: Somewhere private
Music: Rhythmical and relaxing, for example, such as k.d. lang, Gloria Estefan, Marvin Gaye, Govi, Celine Dion. For the remainder of the massage, ambient music – your favourite classical track or recordings of the sounds of nature.
Lighting: Soft, clear lighting
Props: Massage table or bed (if none available this can be done on the floor), sheet or towel, cushions, water-based lubricant, latex gloves, moist towelettes, vibrator, dildo and a small rubbish bin
Partner or friend: Partner required
Note: Short fingernails are necessary, or you can use latex surgical gloves

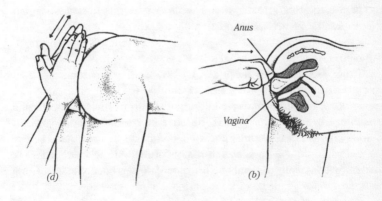

External anal massage. The anus has many nerve endings, so massaging it can be erotic and sensual. (a) Place your palms together and glide them over the anus, as if you were rubbing them together to keep warm. (b) Twist your centre knuckle over the anal bud.

Place the towel or sheet over the surface you are working on. Ask your partner to kneel, or have them straddle their legs either side of you, and place cushions under your partner's body so they can relax. It is important that they are in a comfortable position. With the anal massage, go very slowly and if appropriate wear latex gloves.

With the moist towelettes, gently wipe around the anal bud.
If your partner has haemorrhoids and these are exposed, gently push them inside the anal bud. Use lots of water-based lubricant on your fingers and the palms of your hand and move your thumbs in a circular motion, rotating around the anal bud. With your palms together, place your hands over the anus, gliding them backwards and forwards as if you were rubbing your hands to keep warm. Continue gliding them over the anal bud, allowing the fingers to move over the top to give your partner lots of different sensations. Clench your fist, placing the centre knuckle out slightly and using the knuckle to gently pulse and twist over the anal bud. Using both thumbs either side of the anal bud, stretch and massage it.

At this point you can use a vibrator or dildo externally, in gentle rotating strokes. If you wish to take this massage into anal sex it is advisable to use a dildo first.

After experiencing an external anal massage from his girlfriend for the first time Geoffrey was surprised by his reactions. "I found it to be very nurturing and it was great to be able to let go and enjoy the sensations. I found I connected differently with my partner because it felt more sensual than sexual. Because of the intimacy involved I initially felt very vulnerable, but when I relaxed I was surprised to find how healing the massage was. It really got me in touch with a part of my body I normally see only as functional. When I became aroused it was an intensely pleasurable experience and I now feel much more appreciative of my anal area."

INTERVIEW

PAUL AND GERALD, A GAY COUPLE WHO HAVE BEEN TOGETHER FOR FIVE YEARS

The thing that connects us the most is being able to emotionally communicate, we have gone through a lot of changes in our sexual relationship. We have had times when sex has not worked for us because one of us would lose our erection. Fantasy made it worse because it stopped us connecting with the sensations in our body. It was similar to stage fright. If we set out to have penetrative sex, one of us would feel performance anxiety. We addressed this by watching each other's face during lovemaking and identifying when one of us went into thinking about the sexual experience instead of feeling it. We could tell this by the tension developing in the face.

We tried penile injections to induce an erection, and while they worked, they did not deal with our underlying issues, so we stopped using them. The main thing which has changed how we relate sexually is that we can now be erotic with one another without it ending in penetrative sex. We massage each other, caress and experiment with different Tantric breathing techniques. It is essential to bring the breath and energy from the head back to the navel, to ground ourselves.

This is the best sex either of us has ever had in a relationship because we have learned to discuss our issues. If we go without sex for a while, one of us has to make the effort to initiate it. We both enjoy anal sex, but hygiene is important, so we have a shower and make sure that we have had a bowel movement one hour before. Anal douching gets rid of all the natural flora in the bowel, so we no longer do it. The external anal massage is something we incorporate in our lovemaking and it has allowed us to relax.

6

Pleasurespotting: Answers to the Most Commonly Asked Sexual Questions

I have advised women and men on their sexual pleasure for many years and I continue to marvel at the multi-faceted and complex nature of erotic issues. Many people have traumas around sexuality, with backgrounds of sexual abuse and disempowerment, but they do not have to be stuck in this place. No matter what was experienced in the past you can move beyond it. While you must acknowledge past pain in order to heal, you also need to learn new ways to develop yourself and have fun. Women are great at nurturing other people, but often do not express that same degree of nurturing to themselves. Men can often be good at giving help but find it very difficult to ask for help.

To find out the sexual truth for ourselves, we need to do our own individual emotional and body work and also educate ourselves about sexuality, which is still widely misunderstood. Often a visit to the doctor does not answer your questions on female ejaculation, anal pleasure, how to have a better orgasm. Women's magazine articles on sex are often very simplistic in their approach, leaving out the key questions.

Every woman and man has a different sensual journey, however I have found many similar questions raised about body issues, sexual response, and what is "normal". Here are the questions I have been asked most frequently, in individual sessions, group workshops and by customers in The Pleasure Spot.

Women's sexual pleasure
How can I find my G-spot?
The G-spot was first named by Ernest Graffenberg in the 1940s and has been a controversial subject for many years. It is a cluster of nerve endings and glands which is part of the urethral sponge. Some

people believe it to be the female equivalent of the male prostate. When it is stimulated it can produce a secretion of clear liquid, which is often mistaken for urine. This process is known as female ejaculation.

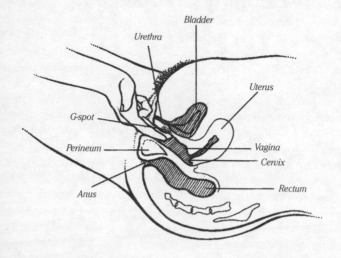

Finding your G-spot: Approximately 5 cm into your vagina you will feel skin with a rougher texture than the surrounding tissue. Your partner can stimulate this point with their finger, pressing it as if it were a doorbell.

To find the G-spot place a finger into the vagina and push it forward towards the stomach. Approximately 5 cm in you will feel skin with a more ribbed or rougher texture than the surrounding tissue. This is the G-spot and it can be anywhere from 2 cm to 4 cm in size. As a woman becomes aroused the tissue swells with blood and it can feel intensely pleasurable.

Encourage your partner to stimulate this point by inserting their finger into your vagina and moving it as if they were ringing a doorbell – in a press/release movement. This technique is more enjoyable than continual pressure. To stimulate the G-spot externally, massage the pubic mound, which is where your pubic hair is located. It also feels good to have the clitoris stimulated at the same time with a finger or an external vibrator.

Some women claim they are unable to feel their G-spot, but I have found during workshops on erotic genital massage that when a woman is relaxed and aroused, there is definitely heightened sexual feeling in the area where the G-spot is located. The Body, Heart and Soul workshops have a wonderful women's G-spot exploration session. Women pair up, and one woman lies on her back, legs apart in a relaxed position. Her partner puts on latex gloves covered with water-based lubricant and gently locates the G-spot. The women then swap over. Explore your G-spot by stimulating it through intercourse, finger insertion, vibrator or dildo play. Some sexual positions, such as "doggie style" are more likely to stimulate the G-spot, so experiment and have fun. A word of warning: if a woman has been sexually abused, trauma can be lodged in the G-spot and stimulating it can bring up emotional pain.

What is female ejaculation?

Female ejaculation does exist! The first female ejaculation I ever saw occurred during a workshop organised by Annie Sprinkle and Joseph Kramer in San Francisco in the mid-1990s. A lesbian woman graciously demonstrated her amazing technique by placing a finger inside her partner's vagina and moving it against the G-spot. I was delighted when I saw the urethral sponge come down from the vagina and be visible as the clear liquid ejaculated. I think all our mouths dropped open, I know mine certainly did.

When the G-spot on the urethral sponge is stimulated, a clear liquid can be secreted. This can occur during regular lovemaking, but seems to be more common when there is G-spot stimulation as well. Not all women will experience ejaculation, it will depend on the style of orgasm she has. The clitoral orgasm has an emphasis on warm energy going up the body, while female ejaculation is a release of energy, with women experiencing a pushing down sensation. To help you learn to ejaculate, use a variation of kegels. Instead of clenching in, gently push out your genital muscles, then relax, then push out again. Repeat this as often as possible, approximately two hundred times a day, to build up the sexual energy in your body. If the wet spot happens to you, enjoy it!

What is the Pubococcygeus muscle?

The Pubococcygeus (PC) muscle is the muscle you use to stop urination mid-flow. It is the muscle you clench and relax when doing kegels; regularly doing these will make your orgasms longer and stronger. I recommend that you do about a hundred of these a day.

You definitely notice the results in a short time.

The PC muscle can be strengthened with duotone balls, which are two hard plastic balls, with smaller, solid ones inside. The balls are tied together with a cord. When you place them inside the vagina the heavier balls rock when you move, encouraging you to clench and relax your PC muscle. Doing housework will never be the same again! An added bonus is that they are wonderful clitoral stimulation. You can ask your partner to stimulate your clitoris and as you are about to orgasm, have them pull out the balls. This stimulates the G-spot and can give you a wonderful orgasm. Small vibrating eggs can also be used internally to strengthen the PC muscle and are lots of fun. If the eggs are not latex covered you will need to use a condom, because any liquid travelling down the cord will affect them. You can also use them externally on the clitoris and as they are so small they are portable and make a great travelling companion.

What are the best sex toys to use?

Vibrators are not new inventions – the first, steam-powered vibrators were patented in the USA in the 1870s. By the early 1900s many physicians were recommending vibrators to their female patients for genital massage, as an aid to good health and relaxation.

Vibrators, dildos and all other sex toys can be used to enhance your sex life whether you are single or have a partner. While demonstrating sex toys on a television programme, I was asked by a man in the audience whether his partner would prefer the toy to himself. I laughed and replied that the vibrator did not have much of a personality, it could not talk to you or take you out to dinner. Some men feel worried that sex toys will detract from their lovemaking, but in reality they enhance it. Women have asked me whether they could become addicted to a vibrator or dildo, and not be able to have sex without it. Sex toys are not addictive. Electric vibrators and massagers are wonderful for relaxing the body, and the more relaxed you are, the more orgasmic you will be. They can be used all over, not only on the genitals.

A good way to start using a vibrator is to begin at the top of the head, placing your hand underneath the vibrator to ease you into the sensations. Continue to work down the body, all the way to your feet, relaxing as you go. For women who want a quiet vibrator, which is not as strong, there is a coil-operated product with attachments on the market. There is a strange myth, which many people believe nonetheless, that electric vibrators can electrocute you. This is completely untrue. Electric vibrators are only used externally, never placed in water and are completely safe. They are sturdy and durable, have strong consistent vibrations and will give you many years of pleasure.

Battery-operated vibrators offer several advantages over electric vibrators: they are inexpensive, portable and have a gentle vibration. Unfortunately, most of them are designed as novelties, have an unpredictable lifespan and can be very noisy. The most common ones are phallic shaped, made of hard plastic and designed to be used externally on the clitoris. Only soft vinyl vibrators should be used internally. A popular vibrator is the butterfly type, which you wear like a suspender belt and which gives clitoral stimulation. While they are more expensive, Japanese vibrators have a sensation all their own. These silicon wonders often have vibrating clit-ticklers, as well as a moving shaft, and pearls which vibrate around the entrance to the vagina where the nerve endings are located. They are the most durable and reliable of the battery vibrators.

Small vibrators, which are designed to fit easily onto a finger, are the ideal choice for someone who has restricted movement in their hands or wrists because of rheumatism, arthritis or RSI. These vibrators are used externally on the clitoris. Another popular vibrator on the market is shaped like a small cactus and can be used internally, both vaginally and anally. The base of this toy vibrates and it feels wonderful on the clitoris.

I am often asked about which dildos I recommend and I specifically like the silicon ones, which I first saw in the USA. I was inspired by their soft texture and beautiful, non-phallic designs. It is fun to use a silicon dildo internally and a vibrator externally on the clitoris, and you can also use dildos to practise kegel exercises. Many of the silicon dildos are curved, which also gives stimulation of the G-spot, and there are silicon dildos specifically designed for anal play.

TIPS: USING A VIBRATOR

Relax your breath, allowing yourself to sigh a few times. Your breath is the key to allowing yourself to relax and have good orgasms.

Using a vibrator will help you to charge your body with sexual energy. Pulse the vibrator backwards and forwards on your genitals, at the same time moving your pelvis. If you bend your knees you will find a gentle rocking motion will take place. If you want to have more fun try doing your kegels at the same time.

Experiment with different positions. You do not just have to lie on your back, you can use a vibrator in all the varied positions you have sex in.

You may find that as you become more excited you want to insert a vibrating or non-vibrating dildo, which will give you a full feeling. There are a wide variety of these on the market. I have found silicon dildos are the best because they are flexible and warm and retain body heat.

If you share your vibrator or sex toy, always remember to put condoms on it. If you alternate between the vagina and the anus, you must use a condom, and you must change this if you move back from your anus to your vagina. It is essential that no bacteria from the anus enter the vagina, as this can lead to vaginal infection.

Although Juliet had always been a sensuous person she had never had an orgasm, either alone or with a partner. She had read many sex manuals and done many exercises to help her become orgasmic but had not been successful and she came to my shop to see if a vibrator could help. She decided to purchase a Japanese vibrator with a clit-tickler, and a butterfly-shaped vibrator. She loved the toys and found that the strong, consistent pressure of the clit-tickler produced an orgasm every time. She told me, 'I had to make a long car trip, and decided to take my new sex toys with me and experiment. I wore the butterfly-shaped vibrator under my clothes and put the other vibrator in my bag. It was the most exciting drive I have ever done! At one stage I got so turned on I had to pull over into a darkened side street, get out my Japanese vibrator and go for it with both hands."

After she had bought the sex toys Juliet asked her partner, Patricia, if she minded if they introduced the vibrator into lovemaking. Patricia was supportive. "Juliet was very honest to bring the issue up and not just hide the sex toys in a drawer. Although the idea of using sex toys with a partner was new to me, I thought if she was brave enough to talk to me about it I should not close my mind to it. It turned out to be a fantastic experience and has really enhanced our relationship."

Samantha and I became friends after she bought her first vibrator at my shop and came back to tell me how it had changed her life. She was in her early forties, had recently split from her husband, and wanted to be able to look after herself sexually, rather than relying on a partner. "I have become sexually confident now because I have tapped into my inner power, which has helped me in non-sexual situations as well. I realise I am a strong and resourceful woman. I love the fact that I can satisfy myself, this has increased my self-esteem and the fun I have in my life. People often ask what's happened to me, and I just smile. I have recently met a new man and he finds the vibrator lots of fun as well."

How can I have better orgasms?
There are many varieties of orgasms: clitoral, G-spot, or breath. Women experience different forms, or combinations, of body sensations which can be classified as orgasms. Many women who have never orgasmed during sexual intercourse worry that there is something wrong with them. There are many important reasons why this might be happening. Some women's clitorises are positioned in such a way that they will only feel stimulated by something external, such as a finger, vibrator, or by oral stimulation. It will also depend on how relaxed and turned on you feel with your partner. For some women it can take twenty to fifty minutes before they feel turned on enough to orgasm. The key to having better orgasms is relaxation and breath. It is important to be aware of your body's sensations, taking time to build up the sexual tension before letting go. Deep breathing allows the body to feel more, and holding your breath stops all sensations. Doing a hundred kegels a day will help improve the quality of your orgasms.

Women and masturbation: how important is it?
The way to have good sex is simple and we all have the answer: start with yourself and become your own best lover. Celebrating who you are means fully accepting and enjoying your body on all its different levels, from the touch of your skin to the sound you make when you are having fun, to the fantasies you create. Sexual relaxation, like everything else, takes time and experimentation, initially with yourself and then if appropriate with another. High self-esteem comes

from enjoying your body, not comparing it to anyone else's. Here are some women's stories to inspire you:

How I found my sexuality again: "I first discovered masturbation at the tender age of thirteen. I was totally bored at school and was able to disguise this with mind-blowing experiences under my desk. The nun who was trying to teach me was oblivious to this and so I was able to merrily masturbate, which was so much more fun than the three Rs. At this time sex was a very taboo subject. I now work with young girls and it is wonderful to see that they can discuss sex openly and without fear. We have certainly come a long way from the days when it was a mortal sin to even think of placing your hands anywhere on your body which caused pleasure. I grew up and married, had two children and a dreadful sex life, which of course eventually led to total breakdown of the relationship. At this point it felt very safe to shut down, which I was able to do without any effort.

"After many years I met through a dear friend a lovely man who was to become my saviour. We became lovers and I played the game of bluff, but he was wiser than I was. Because he was a patient man he taught me how to love using one word – surrender. I did, and at last had my first full body orgasm. We no longer see each other but I will always have a special place in my heart for him."

It's never too late: "After thirty years of not masturbating or having sex because of a sexual trauma, I finally realised in my mid-sixties that I needed to address this issue. I went into a women's sex shop and thought an array of vibrators, dildos, videos and books, and spent the next few months exploring new realms of myself. Under my pillow lives my favourite vibrator and sex toy and at the moment I go to the moon three times a week, which is much better than playing bowls or cards. I never thought life would begin again in my mid-sixties."

Childhood exploration with a friend: "At six years old I was fascinated with genitals. My next-door neighbour, who was the same age as me, would play with and touch himself, in the cupboard. My thrill came one day when I showed him how I masturbated lying on my tummy, rocking back and forth on my hands until I reached amazing sensations, which I later learned was an orgasm. Thirty years later I still use these techniques to have fun."

Most women have been told that masturbation is bad, but it is an essential way to find out what you like and how your body responds. You cannot expect a lover to know what turns you on unless you have done your homework. Some women might feel that masturbation is wrong, shameful or boring, but it is really about you taking time to explore your body in a sensual way.

TIPS: MASTURBATION

Relax your breath, allowing yourself to sigh a few times.

If you want to prolong your orgasms and build up your sexual energy, concentrate on breathing deeply into the belly as you are becoming excited. When you feel ready to let yourself go and relax into having an orgasm, quicken your breathing. Take short breaths into the upper chest, allowing yourself to make sounds as the sexual tension builds up. Sexual sounds are a great way to allow yourself to become more turned on. Kegeling also helps to increase your pleasurable sensations.

It is important to experiment in order to find out what turns you on. Candida Royalle's sensual videos for women, Nancy Friday's and Ruth Ostrow's books on fantasy, and the vast array of vibrators and dildos on the market can help you find out. Feeling sensual, sexual and erotic is about taking time for yourself. This could be dancing, having a bath or a massage, or spending a quiet, loving time with yourself or a lover. Feeling the sensations in your body, and learning what you like so that you can communicate this is vital to having good sex and becoming more orgasmic.

Remember to stroke your whole body, not just your genitals, and pleasure your entire self.

Erotic genital massage, Exercise 5.9, is a great way of relaxing and letting yourself get in touch with what turns you on.

Remember that there will be times when you will feel more orgasmic than others. Stress, tiredness, your state of health and level of anxiety all have a huge influence on how orgasmic you will be.

Look in your diary and set up a date with yourself – this

evening is for you to explore a new realm of your sexuality and the way you would like to be touched. Give the same amount of attention and love to yourself that you would a lover.

Take a mirror and really look at your genitals. Each woman's are different in colour, shape and size. Notice the outer and inner labia, which are the folds of skin on each side of the vagina. You may find that this reminds you of a flower or a shell. At the top of the inner lips you will find the clitoral hood, with the clitoris underneath it. The urethra is the small hole further down where urine comes from, and the anus is below this.

Create an atmosphere in your room when you masturbate – soft lighting, music and essential oils. Start gently touching your body, noticing what feels good and allowing your breathing to become deep and relaxed. The more you breathe, the more you will feel.

As you explore your vulva, try various positions. Some women like lying on their stomach, placing their hands between their thighs, moving backwards and forwards. Others prefer lying on their back, or side. Experiment with pressure, strokes and rhythms, and let yourself feel sensual.

Take time in the bath to play with the shower hose, if you have one.

Teaching your partner the techniques you have learned by yourself will increase the sensual enjoyment of your lovemaking.

What is vaginal fisting?

Fisting is the process of putting all the fingers of your hand into a woman's vagina and then when these are inside her forming a fist. This is a very intense experience and so it is important that there is a significant level of emotional and physical trust between partners. There is no such thing as too much lubricant when fisting and it is best to use a thick one which sticks heavily to your hand. The traditional lubricants used for medical examinations are best and can be bought at a chemist. Apply the lubricant liberally and keep on applying it throughout lovemaking, remembering to cover the whole outside of your hand and down to your wrist. Your nails need to be short and well manicured and you need to keep talking to your partner and letting her direct you. If she is uncomfortable, or feels any level of pain, slow down, remove your hand, take some time out, and, if she wants, try again. Do not rush. The first time you are fisted the sensations are very unusual and can be very scary; many women feel emotional and may cry during or after this type of lovemaking.

Do not make a fist and try to put it inside her. Begin with your middle finger and gradually increase to the three middle fingers; if that feels good, put the little finger inside her. Constantly check in with your partner. Slowly rotate your hand, pushing gently in and out. If necessary withdraw and apply more lubricant, then gently put each of the fingers back inside her in turn. Eventually push your thumb in, which should be tight against the rest of your hand. Do not try to insert your hand in one go. Push your hand in at a slight angle, watching what is comfortable for your partner. You will feel muscle resistance and you might have to move a bit to get your whole hand in, this is all right as long as your partner does not feel any pain. After your hand is inserted fold your fingers into a fist – you might find that you do this naturally.

Your partner may wish you to move your hand slowly around inside her, in and out, part way in and out, or she may wish you to hold your hand still. If she does not tell you what she would like, ask her. It is good at this time to combine fisting with clitoral stimulation, either with your other hand, or with a vibrator. If she orgasms you will feel an amazingly strong muscular contraction. When you are removing your hand, do so very slowly, first unfurling the fist, then slowly pulling your hand out. It is important that you do not hurry.

It might take a number of attempts at fisting to get it right, so be patient if it does not work the first time. Fisting is not for everyone and the fantasy of being fisted may be very different from the reality. Do not be disappointed if you find that it is too uncomfortable.

My partner is bisexual: what issues do I need to be aware of?

Many women are in relationships with bisexual men or women, either knowingly or unknowingly. This can bring up many strong, even conflicting, emotions, such as shock (if they did not know of the partner's bisexuality), anger, sorrow and betrayal. Many men have occasional or casual sex with men, yet they do not identify as gay, or even bisexual. Women should not feel guilty that somehow their behaviour has "caused" this situation to occur, or that their relationship is necessarily over because of their partner's bisexuality. Sexual compromises can be worked out which suit both partners, but sensitivity and good communication are vital. In this situation professional counselling is advised, either at your community or women's health centre, or your local AIDS organisation, which can also help you with safe sex issues.

Pregnancy and menopause: how can I recover my sexuality?

Pregnant women have hormones racing through the body, and for many their libido is very high, maybe much higher than in the past. Yet many people still believe a pregnant woman to be no longer sexual. After recovering from childbirth, and the many sleepless nights which are part of having a baby, women often become concerned that they will never again be a sexual, erotic person.

Marcia came into my shop to buy a vibrator early in her pregnancy. She said she was feeling very horny, masturbating approximately three times a day, but she did not feel like having sex with her husband. A lot of relationship issues were coming up for her and she was angry and jealous. She felt uncomfortable in her body and she only wanted to be touched in a very gentle way, but her libido was very strong. She said that using a vibrator allowed her to go into a feminine space to nurture herself. After the birth of her first child it did not take long for her to feel sexual again, and the issues with her husband were resolved.

INTERVIEW

KENDRA SUNDQUIST, RM MHlth Sc (Ed) MCN, DIRECTOR OF EDUCATION SERVICES, FAMILY PLANNING ASSOCIATION NSW AND THE AUTHOR OF "MENOPAUSE, MAKE IT EASY"

Menopause is a time of physical and emotional changes in the body, as there are hormone imbalances. You can liken it to the hormonal turbulence in puberty as the body winds up for reproduction. Menopause is the winding down. Both take a number of years. The peri-menopausal time can take five to

ten years where women can notice subtle changes in their sexual drive and response. This can start in the late thirties or early forties. Most of the changes are around a five-year period leading up to and before the period stops.

As the body accommodates these changes, it can affect libido and there are different experiences around this. Some women have a heightened sexual response, and at the other end of the spectrum they are not interested. Libido is affected by so many things, like the quality of the relationship, or the fact that the women might not be in a relationship. It takes a woman much longer to get turned on during menopause, due to the changing sensitivity of the skin. Where you once found some thing pleasurable, you now might find it uncomfortable.

Vaginal lubrication also changes, as does the skin around the clitoris and the fatty tissue around the labia. The pubic bone shrinks and sags, exposing the clitoris, which can make it more sensitive. Friction or rubbing on the clitoris can become uncomfortable or even painful. The vaginal wall becomes fine because of less of oestrogen, making micro-abrasions which can bleed during intercourse. Some women find intercourse painful a this time. Menopausal women have to explore alternatives in sexual pleasure: oral sex, masturbation, the joy of a vibrator, or anal intercourse. Women going through menopause are more prone to vaginal infections, so it is essential that no bacteria from the anus goes into the vagina.

It is important for women of this age to be free to explore heir life and sexuality in an uninhibited way, to be brave and look for new adventurous activities. Although orgasms often take longer and are not as intense, they can also last longer; sex might be different but become more pleasurable. It is a journey of exploration and new possibilities.

Men's sexual pleasure

In my work I have found men's sexual issues to be more straightforward, although no less serious. Men's erotic turn-ons are often visual, whereas for women it is more usually other things which stimulate them. One of the biggest breakthroughs I made in understanding men's sexual pleasure was to realise that while women generally like their genitals touched softly, men respond more to a deeper, firmer touch. Women will often touch men the way they want to be touched themselves, and this is usually not as much as a turn-on for the men. Likewise, men will often touch women the same way they like to be touched, and this is often perceived by women as heavy-handed or rough. Men suffer from concern about their body image and the amount of pleasure they can offer a partner just as women do. They also have specific issues which cause them sexual anxiety, such as how to satisfy their partner. Here are some of the most common questions men ask me:

How can I stop premature ejaculation?

Premature ejaculation is the term for coming sooner than you want to and feeling that you have no control. Most men will experience this at least once in their lifetime. When it is only an occasional experience, because you have felt highly excited, a loss of control is not a problem. But when it occurs frequently you may begin to feel you are not able to satisfy yourself or your partner. It may lead to your partner feeling frustrated which can make you feel even more pressured.

An essential part of understanding what is happening is to notice how your body is responding as you get closer to ejaculation. You will find there are different sensations at different levels of arousal. Slowing down and taking time to notice the different feelings cannot only be informative but pleasurable. It is important to be able to talk about sex in a non-sexual situation, because you will feel more relaxed than during lovemaking.

Men have a band of sexual energy around the genitals and therefore most men become very tense when they ejaculate. Relaxation is the key to changing this. As you become turned on, taking easy, deep breaths will allow these sensations to build up more gradually and help you to relax. Moving the hands, arms, legs and feet, even shaking the head, can interrupt the tightening that brings on ejaculation. Some men use sexual fantasies, which have the effect of disconnecting them from their body, making it difficult to delay ejaculation.

The method I advise starts by becoming turned on and concentrating on the feelings and sensations in the body, not disconnecting from it. Bring yourself almost to orgasm and just before you feel you are about to ejaculate, stop touching yourself for a moment and relax, breathing deeply. Repeat this a few times and see how long it takes for the sensations to build up. After about fifteen to twenty minutes allow yourself to come. The fact that you have built up to an orgasm slowly and deliberately will result in a much more enjoyable experience. The next step is to incorporate this stop/start technique into sex with your partner. Some men use a variation of the stop/start method known as the squeeze technique. This is when you grasp the area below the glans between the thumb and forefinger and squeeze for a few seconds.

Often in lovemaking a man can be preoccupied with satisfying his partner and can lose awareness of his own body. This technique allows you to focus on your body sensations, which is essential to changing your sexual arousal pattern. Kegel exercises also help a lot, and I recommend doing a hundred a day. Strengthening the PC muscle gives men more control over their erection, as well as making them capable of feeling more pleasure.

There is an effective Taoist technique which is also helpful for preventing ejaculation.

Marcel who is in his mid-thirties had always suffered from premature ejaculation. His lovemaking normally lasted for an average of three minutes. During our session I explained the above techniques and he incorporated them into his masturbation. When he returned three weeks later he said that he was able to make love for twenty minutes and masturbate for hours without ejaculation.

How can I deal with impotence?

As with premature ejaculation, most men experience impotence at some time in their life, due to age, tiredness, stress, alcohol or drugs. Sometimes it can be caused by physical problems, such as diabetes, cancer, or Multiple Sclerosis, and at other times it can be related to fear or guilt. Impotence can also happen when a man feels pressured to have sex when he really only wants to be held and touched. Or it can have a deeper psychological significance when a man does not want to feel committed to the relationship.

Sexual performance anxiety is often part of the reason for impotency. It is important for the man and his partner to realise that there are many enjoyable things to do which do not require an erection. The flaccid penis is still quite sensitive and enjoys stimulation of all kinds. Massaging and oral stimulation can be pleasurable for both of you, and often when a man no longer feels under pressure his body responds. There is a great deal more to sex than just intercourse, and rather than being goal-oriented, learn to focus on pleasurable body sensations. Deep, easy breathing, communication and kegels are also very valuable.

There are a number of sex toys which can be helpful in producing an erection and one of these is the vacuum pump. Before the pump is used, a specially designed ring made of rubber, leather or metal, generally known as a cock ring, is put around either the base of the penis or the base of the penis and scrotum. These rings are designed to restrict the blood flow from the penis and help maintain an erection. The flaccid penis is placed into the vacuum pump and the pumping action causes it to become engorged with blood. Some men find that wearing a cock ring prolongs their erection or makes their erection firmer; it is important to experiment and find out if this works for you. But make sure the ring is not too tight, and don't wear it for too long, as this can cut off circulation and cause bruising.

There are also injections which can produce temporary erections, but this does not deal with the psychological issues causing impotency. In extreme cases surgical implants can be fitted. Many men find that as they get older and are less able to have erections on demand, they broaden their sexual activities to include more non-genital touch, oral sex, and playing with sex toys. This expands their experience of sensuality and pleasure in more creative ways. Increasing your body sensations, through the exercises in Chapter 2 and Exercise 5.10, can be a wonderful way to pulse erotic energy through the body. This is not reliant on you having an erection. Using a harness and dildo can also be very useful for men who suffer from impotence.

Men and masturbation: how important is it?

Masturbation is something that most males experience by adolescence, and once they have tried it they do it for the rest of their lives. While some believe that masturbation is something you do only when a partner is not available, most men continue to masturbate even when they are part of a couple. Masturbation is not a substitute for sex, it is a wonderful way to experience pleasure and enjoyment in one's own body.

There is no "normal" number of times for a man to masturbate – it can range from three times a day, to once a week, or even once a month. Many men masturbate quickly to release energy and tension in the body, but a better way to experience pleasure is to take time to enjoy the sensations by letting them build up slowly. Be creative and use oil or lubricant on your genitals; set the scene with incense, aromatherapy and candlelight, as this will enhance your self-loving experience. Be daring and masturbate in front of a mirror, or experiment with having an orgasm with your eyes open and closed. Try using different pressure sensations around the testicles and the penis, and stimulate your nipples during sexual play. Masturbating with your partner can give them a greater understanding of your pleasure zones.

Often there are feelings of guilt associated with masturbation which come from adolescence. Communicating your difficult body issues to your partner – "I feel overweight"; "I don't like my shoulders" or "My penis is not big enough" – can be very helpful in a relationship. It will let your partner know what concerns you and therefore what issues arise for you during sex. When we are by ourselves most of us use fantasy to become sexually aroused, but when this becomes the prime focus we become disassociated from our body and it is very difficult to expand sexual pleasure.

Once you have become aroused a wonderful way to heighten your pleasure is to focus your attention on the sensations in your body, and just before you feel you are about to ejaculate, stop touching yourself, relax and breathe deeply. Repeat this three to four times, for about fifteen to twenty minutes, before you ejaculate. Become conscious of how long it takes for the sensations to build up each time. When you are able to get to orgasm slowly and deliberately you will have a much more enjoyable experience.

There are many sex toys for men which can add to your pleasure, such as warm vibrating tunnels, vibrators and anal beads. Incorporating the techniques of full body orgasm – see "Are orgasm and ejaculation the same thing?" – can expand your notion of pleasure. Here are some mens' stories to inspire you:

Rob's first experience: "We often went to my great-aunt's house after church on Sundays. There wasn't much to do there and she and Mum spoke a mixture of German, Polish and Ukranian so that my dad id couldn't follow. I was playing in the tiny front yard, and since there were no trees to climb I decided to climb the clothes pole. There were four poles, about seven feet tall with a little T at the top to wrap the clothes line around. I ran from pole to pole, trying to grab the T. As I shimmied up the third pole, I realised that it felt really, really good.

There was a bulge in my pants and I clung tightly to the steel pole as I ascended so that I would make firm contact with the cool pole. Mum yelled at me to stop so I wouldn't dirty my pants, but I had found a new and wonderful toy."

Getting caught: "We visited my aunt and uncle every summer. I was in the bath on a warm afternoon and got aroused, so I tried my hand at using thick soapsuds to masturbate. It was a very new feeling. I soaped up more and stroked faster and faster, to a fevered pitch. I really wanted to come, and was working up a real sweat with the soap trying to make it happen. Right before I came my uncle walked into the bathroom and saw me with the goods in hand. He simply said, "Oh, I thought you were brushing your teeth," and left. I was mortified, but I long remembered the non-judgemental way he reacted to this act of pleasure."

Viscosity: "I was home sick with a sore throat. As I lay in bed I noticed that my spit was really thick, perhaps a reaction to my inflamed throat I put some on my hand and started rubbing my cock, just around the head, slowly spreading the spit little by little. I donned my clothes and snuck off into the woods behind our house. Leaning against the base of a huge oak tree, I extracted as much spit as I could and bathed my throbbing cock lightly in this self-made lube. I caressed and tried different ways of stroking. This was the first time that I really took my time and experimented. The waves of ecstasy as I ejaculated had me gasping out loud. There was even more pleasure the longer I played. I didn't mind sore throats so much after that."

Does penis size count?

Most men are concerned about the size of their penis at one time or another, if not most of the time. There are many myths about size and most men have difficulty being objective about this. Some of this can be accounted for by the fact that men usually see their own penises from above, and other men's from in front, and this gives the illusion that other men's penises are larger. Look at your own penis straight on in a mirror to get a realistic idea of your size. While there are many jokes about the size of a man's penis, if your partner is not relaxed and comfortable even an average-size penis can feel unsexy.

Penis size is far less important than relaxation and stimulation. The cliché that it is not the size that counts, but what you do with it is actually true. While some people insist they prefer either a smaller or larger size, toning the vaginal or rectal muscles with kegels is more beneficial than trying to find someone of the right size. Focusing on communicating what is pleasurable in lovemaking is much more conducive to good sex than being concerned about penis size.

Are orgasm and ejaculation the same thing?

Male orgasm and ejaculation are often thought to be the same thing. But can one be experienced without the other? Anthony Harden, body worker, answers this question must succinctly.

INTERVIEW

ANTHONY HARDEN, BODY WORKER SPECIALISING IN MEN'T TAOIST SEX TECHNIQUES

Women have the ability to have multiple orgasms, so why not men? I put that question to myself in my mid-thirties during a search for my own sexual fulfilment. The question came up for me because more often than not I had felt a bit let down after ejaculation. Often I had wanted to go deeper and deeper into the sexual experience I was having with my partner, or to keep it going for a much longer period of time and not have it end with ejaculation. I also wanted to experience sexual energy moving throughout my whole body, not just in my cock.

I had been learning meditation for some time and was keen to learn how to use my sexual energy to release tension throughout my whole body, making this a healing experience for myself and a highly stimulating erotic experience for both myself and my partner.

To be able to prolong a sexual experience for yourself is a fantastic feeling. Sex then takes on a different meaning, whether you are with a lifetime partner, someone new, or just want to have extended fun playing with yourself. The aim is the same: to explore and play, taking yourself to higher and higher levels of excitement without falling off the mountain. If you have worked hard to reach a state of sexual ecstasy it makes more sense to stay there and have fun for as long as you want, then you don't just fall off the mountain, you fly.

So how does a man become multi-orgasmic? I had looked at books on the Karma Sutra to give me a clue, but unless I was prepared to spend six months twisting and contorting my body into hundreds of different postures, it seemed like I was going to be unable to get more out of the sexual experience. It all seemed like a hell of a lot of effort, let alone wondering what the other person had to endure.

I then read an article in a men's magazine on the Taoist philosophy of expanding your sexual experience, which stressed keeping it within, rather than just letting it out. It explained the Taoist belief that when a man ejaculates he loses fluids that are vital to the overall well-being of his system. If you can learn to keep the sperm within your body, you will be able to sustain long, hard erections for the rest of your life. This will allow you to make love for hours on end, or until your partner is begging you to stop. I spoke to a friend about the article and he told me he was reading a book called *Multiorgasmic Man*, by Mantak Chia, a master of Taoist sexual energy work. I bought the book and have never looked back.

The Taoist philosophy differentiates between an orgasm and ejaculation. Men are usually taught that these are the same thing. This is not true. An orgasm for a man happens at the point just prior to ejaculation, and by learning a few simple techniques you can prevent ejaculation and push the sensations throughout the body. This leads to an extraordinary sexual feeling and truly creates some amazing results, not only in the body but also in the mind. The Taoist method of sex does not mean tying yourself up in Karma Sutra knots to get to a greater sexual state. It is also non-sexuality specific, so it works as effectively for straight or gay men.

It can give you a new sense of your own physical and sexual power. A lot of men feel guilt about masturbation; generally it is done in a great hurry so as not to get caught. I have come to believe that this is one of the main reasons that men tend to come as quickly as possible during sex, meaning that we miss out on all the subtler experiences to be had along the way. If being able to prolong your own sexual experience and pleasure sounds like something you would be interested in exploring, congratulations.

If you learn to control and prevent ejaculation, you will find that you are able to strengthen your erections so that they are always hard. Even if you have no trouble with impotence, the techniques will help to ensure that you always remain in that very virile state. Even when you are low on energy, these sexual techniques will leave you feeling energised and peaceful instead of depleted.

There are two main areas to work on: the breath, and controlling the PC muscle. We need to learn to contract this muscle to give us more strength and the ability to stop ejaculation.

To learn to separate orgasm from ejaculation, you need to lubricate your penis, or if you are with a partner get them to do it. Start to gently stroke the penis as you would in masturbation. Keep your breath even and pay close attention to how aroused you are becoming. When you feel that you are getting to the point just before ejaculation stop stroking your cock and squeeze down on your PC muscle. As you squeeze down breathe in deeply and imagine the energy travelling up your spine into your head and then down into your navel. This really helps to move the energy throughout your whole body. You will know if you have stopped at the right time because your erection will have gone.

After a few moments begin again, you can do this five or six times and each time you will feel the energy build and move throughout your whole body.

When you have mastered this technique and feel that you have control you can use the PC and breath techniques while entering your partner. You need to thrust and build up the energy to the point just prior to ejaculation, then stop the movement, breathe and squeeze the PC muscle while still remaining inside your partner. If you find remaining inside your partner too stimulating you can withdraw, relax and breathe deeply to move the energy throughout your body. Wait for a minute and begin again.

Once you have mastered these techniques you can remain inside your partner without withdrawal. This means that you will be able to pleasure your female partner to the

point of orgasm, or your male partner for as long as he desires. As with any new technique, mastering it takes time, so relax and enjoy the process. If loss of control over ejaculation happens, don't be disappointed, enjoy the sensations and try again another time.

Pleasure for all
Anal pleasure: what's it about?

Anal eroticism is surrounded by many powerful taboos in our culture and yet millions of men and women find anal play incredibly enjoyable. Pressure and fullness in the rectum feels pleasurable to some men and women, just as vaginal fullness feels pleasurable to some women. Anal penetration can stimulate both the perineal muscle and the G-spot in women, and the bulb of the penis, perineal muscle and prostate gland in men.

Once the anal area is totally relaxed, you may like to insert a finger about 4 cm into the anus. When you press your fingertips against the side, you will feel the two sphincter muscles. The external sphincter is controlled by the central nervous system and you can easily learn to tense and relax this muscle whenever you want. The internal sphincter is controlled by the involuntary or autonomic part of the nervous system, which governs functions such as heartbeat and stress response.

A self-exploratory massage in the shower can help you relax, giving you more idea of how your sphincter muscles work.

If you force your way into the anus it can result in excruciating pain and the body can go into shock. With practice and patience it is possible to gain some control over the internal sphincter, but it will always tense up if you insert too much too soon. The primary association we all have with pressure in our rectum is that we are about to defecate, so it takes some time for the body to adjust to the new sensation. Faeces are not normally stored in the rectum except just prior to bowel movement, but small amounts may remain so anal douching before play can help you feel more relaxed. To douche, get an enema kit from your chemist and follow the instructions with the kit. Douching needs to be done in the bathroom, as you will need a shower recess and easy access to a toilet. Fill the enema bag with lukewarm water and hang the bag higher than your rectum. The nozzle end of the enema needs to be inserted into your anus – use water-based lubricant to make this more comfortable. Take as much

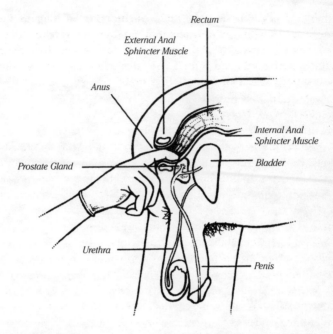

Anal Penetration. Pressures and fullness in the rectum feels pleasurable to some men and women. Do a self-exploratory massage by inserting a finger about 4cm into the anus and feeling the sphincter muscles.

water slowly into your anus as is comfortable and expel it when you need to. Repeat the procedure until the water running out is clear.

The rectum tilts a few inches in towards the front of body, then curves back, sometimes as much as 90 degrees. After a few more inches it swoops back towards the front of the body. It is important to remember this when placing anything into the rectum: 20 cm should be the maximum inserted, otherwise problems can be caused in the intestines. When using anal toys make sure they are smooth and seamless, with a wide, flared base to prevent them being pulled up into the rectum. Anal beads – small beads tied together on a cord – can be inserted into the rectum and pulled out as you are orgasming.

The pleasure derived from being anally penetrated results from the internal massage and a feeling of fullness in the rectum, with many people saying that anal intercourse produces unique sensations of serenity and intimacy. Few people reach orgasms solely from being anally penetrated, so combine this with other genital stimulation. For women this might be a vibrator on the clitoris, or a dildo in the vagina, and for men a massage of the penis and testicles.

TIPS: ANAL PLEASURE

The external skin surrounding the anus has many nerve endings. When these are massaged with oil or lubricant it can be a wonderful way to relax the body and feel sensual. It can take ten to twenty minutes of massage before the body feels relaxed. It is important not to rush anal play, so concentrate on relaxing the breath, inhaling and tightening your pelvic muscles, then exhaling and releasing.

A fun thing to do is introduce toys externally during the massage. Try things with a soft, smooth surface like rubber, silicon dildos, butt plugs and vibrators. Intermingle these with rotating thumbs, fingers and knuckles, but make sure your fingernails are filed smoothly. It is easy to scratch or tear the tissue of the rectum and then for bodily fluids to pass from the rectum into your bloodstream. See Exercise 5.11 for more ideas.

Remember when using condoms and vinyl gloves that most of them are not compatible with oil-based lubricants, so make sure you use a water-based one and lots of it. The anus and rectum do not produce any natural lubrication. Latex or vinyl gloves also have a great soft feel in the anus and are easy to dispose of when you have finished. When sharing toys always use condoms and change them between partners.

When playing anally with women, be aware not to take any of the massage strokes or toys from the anus to the vagina because this can cause a bacterial infection.

Oral sex, or rimming, can be enjoyed by placing a length of non-microwaveable clear wrap or a dental dam, against the anus. Using lubricant on the inside of the wrap or dam against the anus feels great.

The most common techniques for anal play include touching

the anal opening with a finger while masturbating, or stimulating a partner's anus during intercourse or oral sex. Try moving your finger in gently, leaving it in until the anus relaxes, then moving it in and out in a circular motion.

Doing kegels strengthens not only your PC muscle but also the anal sphincter.

Renee experimented with anal sex with her partner Karla. We had only been together for a short time when during our sexual play the issue of anal sex came up. We all know about genital sex, but when you start to play anally it requires a lot more trust and sensitivity, because it is traditionally a sexually taboo subject and we carry the tension around this in our body. I find that anal sex is a very intense sensation and it is a glorious feeling to give and receive anal pleasure. When I first stimulate my partner's anus it is very tight and the muscles grip my finger, but as she gets closer to orgasm her anus relaxes and opens. It is one of the most intimate and loving things you can do with a partner, and when we make love this way it gives me goose bumps all over my body. Anal sex requires good hygiene, so we always use latex gloves and lots of lubricant."

What are the dos and don'ts of piercing?
When you are having your nipples pierced you must have them measured before the piercing, as they will swell afterwards. This affects the choice you make about nipple jewellery; often wearing barbels is more comfortable on a daily basis, with rings worn on a special occasion.

For women, having the clitoral hood pierced is very popular and gives a lot of stimulation. While a clitoral piercing is very pleasurable, if the clitoris is too small it can have difficulty in healing.

Labia piercing has a long history, first used many hundred of years ago, with rings on each side of the labia padlocked as a means of imposing chastity. Now this is purely decorative. Labia piercing should be done above the vagina, and it is important, if you are having more than one piercing, not to place them opposite each other, as this can cause irritation.

Penis piercing in men is done for decoration and pleasure, with the most common one called a Prince Albert, named after Queen Victoria's husband who had such a piercing. In this a ring is pierced through the underside of the fraenulum, the sensitive place below the head of the penis, and comes out through the eye of the penis. This gives pleasurable sensations as the ring rubs against the inside of the urethra, which is lined with nerve endings, and during lovemaking.

The ampallang is a horizontal barbel placed through the head of the penis, which also creates many pleasurable sensations for a lover. In Borneo all men are expected to have them to delight their partner. With this piercing it is important never to pierce through the shaft of the penis, as it contains two large blood vessels which, if punctured, will not allow the penis to become erect.

What do I need to know about safe sex?

Semen, blood, vaginal fluids and breast milk are all potentially HIV infectious and can contain enough of the virus to transmit to another person. So if you are having unprotected sex – sex without a condom or a dam – then there are degrees of risk for the transmission of HIV, as well as other sexually transmitted diseases (STDs). Don't wait until you are in bed, in the heat of the moment, before you bring up safe sex. Many people think discussing safe sex in advance is unromantic, but you have to take up the challenge – your health is paramount.

If you have been in a long-term relationship with your partner and you wish to stop having safe sex, both partners can agree to be tested for HIV (and other STDs), then continue to have safe sex for three months, which is the window period for the virus to develop to detectable levels, then be retested. Pre-test and post-test counselling should be included in this process.

Oral sex, whether on a man or woman, is considered to be low risk, but the degree of risk is increased if the partner who is performing oral sex has bleeding gums, ulcers or cuts in their mouth. It is important to be aware of oral hygiene and if you are concerned about these areas it is better to use a latex barrier – either a dam, which is a square of latex that can be used for oral or anal sex, or a condom.

Withdrawal as a safe-sex strategy is not safe. HIV has been isolated in "pre-come" – the fluid which sometimes comes out of a man's penis prior to ejaculation. As you cannot tell by looking at anyone if they have any kind of STD, safe sex is a necessity with any unknown sexual partners. Condoms come in all sizes, colours and textures, and waterbased lubricants come in many different flavours. Safe sex can actually make your sex life more interesting, playful and exciting. Worrying about whether you are getting an STD is not very erotic, or romantic. Knowing that you are protected allows you to be relaxed and comfortable about the sex you are having.

Kissing does not transmit HIV. Although HIV has been isolated in saliva, you would have to swallow a swimming pool full of saliva before you could get infected. If you do not know the HIV status of the person you are having sex with and you have cuts or wounds on your body, cover them with band aids; if your hands are cut you could wear latex gloves. This may seem very clinical, but gloves can take on a different meaning if you make putting them on an erotic, playful encounter.

Unprotected, penetrative anal sex is high risk for HIV, and any unprotected sex with people who do not know their HIV status is risky. How many people know the HIV status of the people they are having sex with? We must develop the sexual language and confidence to talk about these issues. This may not be easy, especially for women, but it is empowering. For more information, go to your GP if you are confident of their knowledge and you are comfortable talking to them, or to a sexual health clinic or your local AIDS Council.

Sexual challenges: dealing with a disability

The attitudes and values of family, society or carers impact enormously on the sexuality of people with disabilities. People who are intellectually, psychologically or physically disabled are viewed either as sexless creatures or people whose sexuality is out of control. In reality the main problems are a lack of privacy for people to engage in consenting sexual activity, a lack of information about how their condition impacts on their sexuality, and a lack of access to suitable resources.

Many carers of people with an intellectual disability consider their sexual behaviour to be troubling, most commonly public masturbation. Their behaviour is looked at in isolation and attempts are made to modify it, but it would be more useful to look at what needs are being met by that behaviour and to help develop a more appropriate way to meet those needs. Often people caring for the disabled wait for a sexual issue to come up before discussing sex, rather than initiating discussion first. There is still often hesitancy in showing sexual videos and providing sexual material to people with disabilities. Teaching in this area is best if it is pro-active, rather than waiting until behaviours become problematic for other people. When medical histories of people with disabilities are taken and their physical condition charted, this needs to include their sexual history as well.

Sex education for the disabled should cover the three dimensions of sexuality: reproduction, socio-emotional and physiological. The most important dimension is the socio-emotional one, with the most crucial aspects of that being self-esteem and attitudes and values. If these are positive and solid, then if anything untoward happens in other areas of life, it will be possible to deal with them.

Matthew was an intellectually disabled sixteen-year-old boy whose carer was concerned about his public sexual behaviour, particularly his habit of rubbing his genitals up against fences, doorways and posts. The carer wanted to know how to stop this behaviour. A sexual counsellor spoke to the carer extensively about Matthew's relationship with his body and learned that Matthew had a reluctance to touch his penis at any time, even when urinating. This habit had developed when he was quite young, after he had been caught masturbating and been physically punished. He had formed a belief that he should not touch his genitals, but at sixteen with hormones racing through his body, he needed some sort of touching and physical relief. The counsellor worked with Matthew and his carer to unlearn all his negative early messages about his genitals and replace them with positive ones.

In her late thirties Jenna had a physical accident which left her with no feeling from her waist down. She had been happily married for twelve years and was concerned about how this injury would affect her sexual relationship with her husband – it was important to her that this continue. She concentrated not on what she had lost, but on what she could use to replace it, and on enjoying the sensations she still had. After much experimentation she realised she could still feel every physiological sensation of orgasm, but now this was located at the back of her neck. She had orgasms this way and they were very satisfying.

INTERVIEW

TUPPY OWENS, UK SEX WRITER, EDUCATOR AND COUNSELLOR SPECIALISING IN WORKING WITH PEOPLE WITH DISABILITIES. SHE IS THE ORGANISER OF THE SEX MANIAC'S BALL, WHICH RAISES MONEY FOR SERVICES FOR PEOPLE WITH DISABILITIES.

The most difficult issue for people with disabilities is getting in touch with their sexuality. Most people with disabilities have negative images about themselves and often think that their body has such defects that nobody will ever desire them, or that they are hideous or sexually inadequate. Some lucky disabled people manage to reject these views. If you have a lively, erotic imagination and can find ways of pleasuring yourself, this will help to overcome the negativity. This pleasure can easily be shared with another and bring mutual delights and joy.

If your disability is very obvious to people who meet you, you have to develop your own approach to socialising and finding sex partners. Even if people are initially put off by your appearance, they may have experienced bad relationships and be seeking deeper, more meaningful ones. They may be willing to look beneath the external surface and discover that people with disabilities still have true erotic potential. They might not want to marry you because of what their parents and peers will think, but they may find you an exotic sexual adventure. Then you have the chance that love will keep you together, privately if not publicly!

Practicalities may make it difficult for some disabled people to be in touch with their sexuality: short or inactive arms may make genital masturbation impossible. Visual impairment may confuse erotic imagery. Hearing impairment may isolate people so that they do not know there are places to go to enjoy voyeuristic or exhibitionist experiences where speech is unnecessary. A general lack of communication may frustrate a disabled person who is gay and does not know there are gay and lesbian communities they can be part of.

My tips include throwing caution to the wind and stating

your sexual desires. People will be pleased to know that you want to find lovers, and that you are prepared to take risks. The bigger the risks you take, especially if done with a sense of humour, the more likely you are to find sex. It is important to remember that everyone gets rejected, and the loss is as much to the person who rejects you as it is to yourself. If you view the mating game more as a game than an emotional drama, you will do better. Having some friends to laugh with over rejections helps enormously. Accept yourself. Pleasure yourself. There is nothing as off-putting as a panting, frustrated, strange-looking person chasing you. Never be that person. Be cool and skilled.

7
Sensational Sex: How to Spice Up your Sex Life

This chapter is about having fun, expanding a side of yourself you did not know existed, whether you are by yourself, in a long-term relationship, or you want to experiment with a close friend. The techniques and exercises explored here will enlarge your ideas about fantasy, striptease, domination and submission, and even having fun with food. Being creative, having fun, taking chances and exploring your sexual creativity will add a new playful dimension to your life.

Striptease
We are all erotic beings and it is important for us to express this and have fun. Elizabeth Burton has been an erotic dancer and striptease artist for thirty years, working in films, dance troops and plays. She now gives classes for women who want to learn to strip. I saw her strip when she was in her late forties and she inspired me with her natural sensuality and grace. I started organising courses run by Elizabeth for ordinary women who wanted to learn to strip for their lovers or for themselves. The courses have been hugely successful and are usually booked out in advance. They offer women the opportunity to explore their bodies in a safe environment.

Says Elizabeth, "I want women to appreciate that their body is perfect for them, regardless of its shape or size. We get so much negative programming about our bodies as women and I want them to love the body they live in. Deep eroticism comes from within, we are all goddesses inside. I have performed for many years and also taught stripping classes to women, men and mixed groups. For men some of the moves are obviously different, more masculine, but the routine comes from the same place. We all only have one body and we need to love it and look after it."

Consider the type of stripper you might like to be and do not allow yourself to be limited to stereotypes. Why not be a sexy check-out chick, a nightclub torch-singer, a cowgirl, a leather biker, a police officer, or a French maid? For extra impact consider hiring an outfit for the night, but if this is not possible improvise with what you have at home. The right props can help set the scene and allow your stripping persona to emerge naturally. For a glamorous look wear a long slinky dress, gloves, costume jewellery, boa, high-heels, stockings and a wig. For a biker girl wear leather, cut-off jeans, boots, studs and chains, bandana and fake tattoos. A French maid needs an apron, gloves, high-heels, stockings, lingerie and a feather duster. For a policewoman don a uniform jacket and hat, handcuffs, heavy boots and a toy gun.

Let yourself get totally into the persona – the more you go into the character, the easier you will find it to be erotic. Do kegels to connect with the sexual energy in your body.

You can make a cheap outfit out of pantihose. Cut off the legs below the knees for pedal pushers, or at the top of the thigh for short shorts. For a sexy top, cut out the crutch of your pantihose, making a hole large enough for your head, and cut off the feet. Pull the pantihose over your head through the hole you have cut in the crutch area. Slide your arms through the legs and push your hands out where the feet have been cut off. You now have a sexy sheer top. Or you can cut the legs off pantihose and use them as gloves: cut the feet off and make a hole for your middle finger, hook your finger through and roll the stocking leg up your arms. Pantihose outfits can be torn off by you or your partner without worrying about ruining an expensive outfit.

Exercise 7.1 offers a suggested stripping routine. If you find it difficult to strip as yourself, create a stripping persona and give yourself a stripper's name, such as Silver, Pepper, Babette: use your imagination. Practise your routine with your costume and music a couple of times by yourself before you do a performance for a friend or lover. This will help build your confidence. You do not have to have a partner to have fun with stripping – invite a close friend over for an evening where you strip for each other. Nor do you have to remove all your clothes to be a good stripper, often it is what you do not take off that is most erotic.

EXERCISE 7.1: STRIPTEASE FOR WOMEN

Time: Half an hour

Setting: Somewhere you will feel comfortable

Music: Up-tempo, sexy tracks, such as Prince, Madonna, or Tina Turner. Or consider sensual, seductive music, such as Frank Sinatra, Nina Simone or Nat King Cole. Belly-dance music is also suitable.

Lighting: Soft and sensual – dim the lights or use lamps or candles.

Props: Wigs, high-heels, underwear, gloves, costume jewellery, scarves, feathers. The more layers you wear, the better. Keep your audience guessing as long as possible!

Partner or friend: Optional

(a)   *(b)*

Striptease for Women. Consider the type of stripper you might like to be and let yourself go into the persona. (a) Enter the room, stroking the door and leaning against the doorframe. (b) Wiggle your body, run your hands through your hair and down the front of your body, lowering your eyes.

Start by closing your eyes, turning on the music and saying to yourself, "I am a wonderful, sexy woman." Enter the room, stroking the door and leaning against the doorframe. Make eye contact if your partner is there. Prance into the room, freeze, go down to your ankle and stroke up your leg, stopping at the hip and rocking to the music. Wiggle your body. Run your hands up through your hair, down the front of your body and over your breasts, lowering your eyes as you do so. Look up at your partner.

Start unbuttoning or unzipping a piece of clothing, or remove a glove or necklace. Swing it and throw it to your partner. Strut, imagining you are a catwalk model, then freeze. Rock your hips, feeling the sexual energy surge through your body. Slide up to your partner and get them to undo the next layer. You can tease them by pointing to what you want them to remove and, as they put their hands out to you, quickly pulling out of range and wiggling your finger at them. Start undoing the garment yourself, then come in closely and let them take it off.

Go back to the doorframe and dance. Bend down from the waist with your bottom to the audience and wiggle. Use the door to support yourself.

Do a breast tease by gripping your left hand on your right wrist and your right hand on your left wrist. Push back and forward, this will make the breasts move by moving the muscles underneath your arm.

Wiggling your body down, sit on the floor, legs outstretched and toes pointing. Your elbows or hands should be against the floor, propping up the top half of your body. Roll on one hip and caress your bottom.

Take off your shoes and remove your stockings, sensuously rolling them down your legs. Hold the stockings between your big toe and first toe, extend your leg, point your toe, pull your leg back and let the stockings fly.

Lie flat on your back on the floor and arch your back like a cat stretching. Turn over, and with your arms outstretched to support your upper body, move your hips up and down, doing pelvic bounces. Slide to a kneeling position, caressing your breasts and inner thighs. Lean back, rotating your pelvis and caressing your body.

Gracefully stand, and moving to the music remove the last of your garments. You can use a long feather or scarf in a peek-a-boo manner, showing just what you want to show.

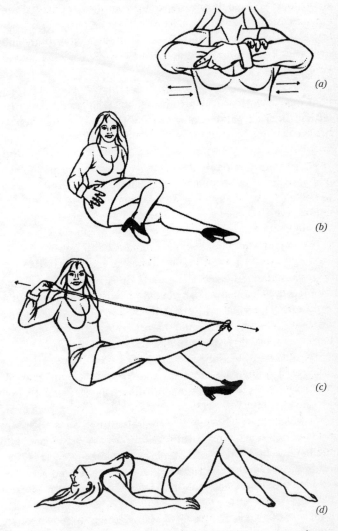

Striptease for Women. (a) Do a breast tease. (b) Roll on one hip and caress your bottom. (c) Hold your stockings between your toes, extend your leg, point your toe, pull your leg back and let the stockings fly. (d) Lie on your back and arch like a cat..

TIPS: STRIPPING

Make sure you have some uninterrupted time. Create a sensuous environment with aromatherapy, using essential oils such as ylang ylang, patchouli, rose or neroli.

When you are stripping, eye contact is essential. Throughout the strip, freeze every so often and just look seductively at your partner.

Remember the "tease" in striptease; tantalise your partner by letting them see a side of you they might never have seen before.

Touching and stroking yourself is a real turn-on for yourself and your partner. Stripping is about having fun, so remember to smile (or even laugh) during your performance.

Wearing high-heels is an added bonus as they give you a natural extra wiggle.

Veronica, in her mid-thirties, came to do the stripping workshop after her long-term relationship had ended. Her partner had been Very sexually critical of her and she felt she was not an attractive or desirable woman. She knew this was not true and she wanted to free up her inner sensuality, which had been crushed by her ex-partner. It Took her a while to feel comfortable in the class, but the support of other women helped her to relax and move with the music. She started to have fun and said to me, "This is the best time I have had in ten years".

Sheree wanted to give her husband a surprise on their twentieth wedding anniversary, so she did a striptease course and after a candlelight dinner gave him an evening he will never forget. "This was a wonderful alternative to buying a present. It reminded my husband that twenty years after our wedding I am still a sexpot who can turn him on like no-one else."

Lauren had always been a large woman, conscious of her weight, and this had left her always feeling disconnected from her body. Her New Year's resolution was to accept her body as it was and bring out the fleshy fan-dancer within. At the workshop she took on the persona of a nightclub singer, bringing with her a newly acquired boa and a red, slinky evening dress. She developed a routine that delighted her, and changed the way she saw herself.

Men too can titillate their partner by stripping, taking on characters as diverse as a sexy executive in a business suit, a spy in a trench coat, a smouldering officer in a military uniform, a bad-boy biker, or a construction-site stud. Many of the tips and suggestions in the exercise for women are applicable to men too.

EXERCISE 7.2: STRIPTEASE FOR MEN

Time: Half an hour
Setting: Somewhere you will feel comfortable
Music: Up-tempo, sexy tracks, such as Prince, Madonna, Michael Jackson, Tina Turner, Whitney Houston, Bruce Springsteen, Sting. Or consider sensual, seductive music, such as Frank Sinatra, Nina Simone, Nat King Cole, Harry Connick Jnr. Belly-dance music is also suitable.
Lighting: Soft and sensual – dim the overhead lights or turn them off and use lamps or candles
Props: Clothing appropriate to the persona you are creating. The more layers you wear, the better. Keep your audience guessing as long as possible!
Partner or friend: Optional

Start in the doorway, walk strongly into the room, rotate your hips and give your partner a wink. Strut forward with your hands hooked in braces, or around your coat lapel, or in your singlet. Thrust your pelvis forward. If you are wearing a jacket, drop it over your shoulders, halfway down your back, and give your partner another wink and a smile. Drop the jacket to the floor. Turn around and look back over your shoulder, rocking your hips back and forth.

Have fun as you remove layers of clothing. Make undoing your belt and your tie as slow and erotic as possible. Sensuously undo any buttons or zips.

Disrobe the upper body. Touch yourself all over, focusing on the part of your body your partner likes best; this may be your arms, legs, bottom, shoulders. Grab that part of the body firmly and look at your partner sexily.

Run your hands through your hair, over your head, or hold

your hat if you are wearing one. Tease your partner, and do not take your erotic emphasis straight to your genitals. Give your partner lots of attention and show them the show is for them.

When you remove your pants, face away from your partner and bend down, rocking your bottom back and forth. Undo one shoe and slip your finger into your sock, slipping them both off in one smooth movement. Do the same on the other side.

Get your partner to help you remove the final pieces of clothing.

Striptease for Men. Take on any character, from an executive in a business suit to a bad-boy biker. (a) Throw your jacket over your shoulder and give a wink and a smile. (b) Look back over your shoulder, rocking your hips. (c) Take off your clothes as erotically as possible.

Fun with fantasy

An element of fantasy is tied into our daydreams as well as our creativity, but fantasy becomes detrimental when we cannot distinguish, between it and reality. Fantasies have their foundation in our childhood, drawing on make-believe, role-playing and real-life experiences. Verbal and non-verbal information is picked up on many levels as sexual or sensual messages filter through our parents, siblings, peers, movies, magazines and books. As we sexually mature, our fantasies become more explicit, as well as a way of exploring ourselves safely.

The positive functions of fantasy are to increase sexual desire and orgasm, enhance self-esteem, relieve stress and tension, and help us cope with past traumas. Healing can happen through sexual fantasies, where we can imagine ourselves feeling more pleasure and fulfilment, as well as having the sort of relationships we want in our life. Fantasies can also help us develop a new level of trust around love and caring, instead of the abuse or hurt we might have experienced in the past. Becoming conscious of our fantasies and their themes can be a way of unlocking fear and negative self-image. As we explore our fantasies we can see that the plot changes, but there is often a similar theme and power dynamic. Unwanted fantasies are often about unresolved hurt, not perversion, and as we unravel the meaning we see the need for love, safety and trust.

Fantasies are not always about wanting to create a particular scenario in real life: a rape fantasy is not about someone wanting to be raped, it often means wanting to be able to give up control. On a detrimental level, fantasy can be a way for us to remove ourselves from our body sensations, a means of blocking emotional intimacy. Becoming less dependent on unwanted fantasies – by concentrating on your breath, body, and feelings of closeness and connection – can allow a depth of sensuality. Give yourself permission to explore new realms: masturbating or making love with your eyes open, making sounds and using different positions. Developing aspects of our fantasy life enriches pleasure.

INTERVIEW

RUTH OSTROW, AUTHOR OF "HOT AND SWEATY" AND "BURNING URGES"

There are as many different fantasies as there are stars in the sky. Sharing your fantasies can be a good marital tool, and, according to my research, people who share their fantasies have a hot sex life, as they see their partner as a

sexual creature and not just a domestic person. Most people have fantasies and they are all expressed in different ways. Visual erotic images are a turn-on for some, while others will have huge story lines and a Cecil B. De Mille cast of thousands. Someone who is into touch will be turned on by the fantasy of being caressed. Some fantasies will be triggered by a certain type of dialogue. There is no norm.

Exercise 7.3 is about exploring the origin of your fantasies and eroticism. You are the only person who can decode your sexual fantasies, but to unlock them you will have to trust your intuition. This exercise is not about being ashamed, embarrassed or judgemental, it is about helping you to discover more about yourself.

EXERCISE 7.3: DISCOVERING YOUR FANTASIES

Time: Over a period of one to two weeks
Setting: Somewhere you will not be disturbed
Music: None
Lighting: Natural
Props: Exercise book, pens, coloured pencils or markers
Partner or friend: Not required

Write down your sexual fantasies over a period of one to two weeks. In a non-sexual situation, analyse the plot and characters as you would a play or TV series. If you are visual, drawing and writing down what the characters are saying or feeling is helpful. It can help to use role-play with dialogue.

Take special note of how the characters interact in the fantasy with regard to your self-esteem and self-acceptance; the level of harm, violence, anger and danger; and the issue of control. Are you either out of control, or controlling the situation? Consider the correlation between the fantasy and your real life, especially around intimacy and sexual stimulation.

When you have looked at the different themes and elements, ask yourself:

• Which of these would you like to use to enhance your sex life?

• What areas need to be healed? What do the sensations or images remind you of?
• What stories recur in your fantasies?
• What makes the story erotic? Expand on the characters' intentions and desires, and as you do, focus on what your needs are in the present.

You can use the information from this exercise as a basis to heal, by expanding your fantasies to include more of what you want in your life. You can change and develop the plots, go in and out of the fantasy, or stop it if you feel it is detrimental. Perhaps not using a fantasy during lovemaking and using it during masturbation might be a way for you to explore pleasure. If you feel there is a sufficient level of emotional safety, sharing your sexual fantasies can bring you closer to your partner. I have spoken to many couples who share their stories, or make new ones up together, as a way of inspiring one another, creating more intimacy and spicing up their sex life.

Sometimes taking elements or roles from fantasies and acting them out can add a new and stimulating dimension to lovemaking, an element of erotic fun and playfulness. The roles you take on can be based on fictional characters – Superman and Lois Lane, Robin Hood and Maid Marion, Batman and Robin – or they might be based on classical roles – soldier and officer, nurse and patient, animal handler and dog, fireman and arsonist, prostitute and client, customs officer and drug smuggler or Victorian governess and student. Fantasy role-play can also involve changing gender, cross-dressing, or being a different age. The sexual tension in role-playing is based on eroticising the interactions between characters. Once you get into a role you will find this is very easy to do.

Most people do have a secret erotic fantasy scenario and this is often what we think of when we are masturbating. Some fantasies are just too elaborate or even dangerous to re-enact, but many could playfully be incorporated into sex with a trusted partner. You might also be pleasantly surprised at the sort of fantasies your partner has locked away. Before you re-enact any fantasy, discuss it thoroughly with your partner. Do not wait until you are in the middle of acting out a fantasy to negotiate it, or you could find the whole experience not working for either of you. Decide what your limits are: How far are you prepared to go into your role? What sexual and non-sexual acts are off-limits? How will you signal to your partner that you do not want to continue with the fantasy?

Putting the time in beforehand to ensure you do not cross either partner's emotional or physical boundaries will help you have a safer and sexier experience. Do not be pressured into acting out any roles which make you feel embarrassed or ill at ease. The point is to have fun, not to get upset or offend anyone.

TIPS: CREATING A SUCCESSFUL FANTASY

You can really enhance a fantasy by doing some research, so that you know how your character would behave. Read books or magazines, or watch films or videos to give you an insight into characters, real people or historical periods.

Work out before you start how much time you have and structure your fantasy accordingly. It is very unsatisfying to have to suddenly end a great role-play because your private time has run out.

It is important to look as much like the character you are creating as possible, to put you into the role and allow your partner to see your persona. This makes it easier to move into the emotional creation of the character. Your partner needs to dress up as well, as fantasy role-plays will not work if only one person is in role. This does not mean spending a fortune on costumes; you can sew them, or scan second hand shops for suitable items. Do not underestimate how much scarves, ties, belts, shoes, gloves and costume jewellery can change an ordinary outfit into a fantasy costume.

You need to be in role straight away at the beginning of the fantasy, because this helps to get your partner into the role. If you are doing a medical fantasy, for example, where you are the doctor and your partner is the patient, begin by asking if they parked in the medical centre's car park, or if they know where to get their prescriptions filled. This general chat moves you both into the fantasy, helps you get into character. Although you are having fun, take your role seriously, and stay in it for the duration of the fantasy.

Try to make the physical environment as much as possible like the fantasy environment. Be inventive and let your imagination go. A dining table with a white sheet thrown across it can become a medical examination table. Your kitchen can become an office staff room, or a military mess; your bathroom can become a prison shower.

Use appropriate language and terminology. Don't make references to phones or faxes if you're recreating the eighteenth century.

Find a role which suits you, perhaps involving a part of yourself you would like to play with and develop. You need to be able to maintain the persona for the duration of your play time, so think about this before you start. Do you have only ten minutes of "naughty school boy" in you? If so this will be very unsatisfying for your partner if they wish to play being a stern headmistress or master for a couple of hours.

Do not just stop the role-play abruptly and go back into your real self. Bring your fantasy to some sort of natural conclusion, with maybe one of you leaving and coming back later, out of role. Decide beforehand how you will end, so that both partners know it is over. Often people end the play with lovemaking, the fantasy having built up delicious sexual tension.

Maggie and Robyn incorporate fantasy role-play into their relationship as a way of freeing the inner child. Maggie explained, "We have fantasy games while making love to allow our inner child into our sex lives, making us not just partners and lovers, but playmates as well. A lot of our sexual activity is about playing, with pirate scenes being our favourite. It is something which has developed slowly within our relationship. We went from one fantasy game to another and found characters we liked. Sometimes we just play the characters themselves, at other times we flesh out a whole story to go with the characters. This heightens the sexual tension and we try to use all of the senses when we recreate a fantasy. It is easier to play with fantasy when there is less pressure and fewer demands in your life, so weekends are easier than weeknights. Although this has allowed our sex life to expand and grow, I do not believe it is good to play sexual fantasy games if one of you is feeling sensitive or vulnerable. If you are having a negative response to something, communicate this honestly to your partner."

Exercise 7.4 is about having fun with your partner and letting them see you in a new way. You are to change your looks and invent a new name and past for yourself.

EXERCISE 7.4: THE BLIND DATE

Time: An evening
Setting: In an appropriate social situation
Music and lighting: Will be determined by your destination
Props: See below
Partner or friend: Partner required

Both of you need to buy or hire a new outfit, change your hair colour or wear a wig – change your look in some dramatic way.

Be creative. Meet your partner at a restaurant, bar or club which is not one you regularly frequent. When you meet, pretend you are strangers meeting for the first time, on a blind date, and play the game of seduction with one another. You will find out things about your partner that you never knew.

Lillian and her boyfriend Paul decided to have an extra-special New Year's Eve, so instead of going to a party they played at being sexy strangers in an out-of-town bar. Lillian arrived first and perched herself on a bar stool in a short, black velvet dress. Soon there was a whisper in her ear, "Are you here alone?" She turned to see Paul, who was dressed not in his usual jeans and T-shirt but in a pair of smart black pants, crisp white shirt and leather vest. The evening was a great success, with both of them playing their new roles to the hilt. They saw a new side of each other, a turn-on for them both.

EXERCISE 7.5: FUN WITH FOOD

Time: An evening
Setting: Home environment
Music: Something you both like, anything from classical to rock 'n' roll
Lighting: Clear for cooking, dimmed or candlelight in the bedroom
Props: Food to cook with, a plastic sheet or a large beach towel for the bed
Partner or friend: Partner required

Start in the kitchen, with you and your partner cooking a meal together, fully dressed. Make sure it is food you both enjoy and that you are very physically connected while you are creating the meal – stir the food together, or hug your partner from behind while they stir. Take the completed meal to the bedroom, where the plastic sheet or towel has been laid on the bed. Start to feed each other. For each mouthful of food an article of clothing is to be removed, so it is good to be wearing many layers as this increases the sexual excitement. When you are naked use your lover as a plate to eat from, but be careful of hot food on naked flesh.

Sensuous, sweet food is particularly wonderful for this exercise: mangoes, strawberries, cream, chocolate and champagne. Put food on your lover's chest or breasts, shoulders, stomach, legs, feet, down the spine or on the back of the neck, paying attention to the areas they find particularly erotic. One great tip is to put something cold, such as ice cubes, on your lover's nipples while you sip a warm drink. When they cannot stand the cold any longer, put your warm mouth over their cold nipples – this feels wonderful!

It is important not to put food inside anyone's genitals as this can cause infection. If you want to eat food from a woman's genital area, eat from her pubic mound. Make sure juices from food do not go into the eye of a man's penis.

Kim-Maree has had many memorable times combining food and sex. "A couple of years ago I was in the kitchen with my girlfriend making spaghetti sauce, which was splattering over the front of me. I took off my shirt to save it and my girlfriend dipped her fingers in the sauce and smeared it over my breasts. We started laughing and she began to lick the sauce off. I then pulled her T-shirt off and rubbed sauce over the front of her, then removed it with my tongue. Before we knew it, we had grabbed the spaghetti sauce and headed to the bedroom. All I can say is we didn't get back to the kitchen that night to make the pasta, and it is still the best spaghetti sauce I ever tasted!"

Sensory deprivation

Some of my most intense spiritual and sexual experiences have involved sensory deprivation with lovers or during workshops. Sensory deprivation involves removing the senses – sight, sound, smell, touch and taste – one by one and then reintroducing them. Removal of one sense heightens the remaining senses, making them more easily aroused. If you are blindfolded your sense of hearing is heightened, because you now use it to listen for information you would automatically take in visually. When you are in soft bondage and unable to move, every touch becomes more intense. In a flotation tank, suspended in the dark in water, you are forced to think differently about your sense of sight and also the feeling of gravity.

You can have a lot of fun removing your partner's or a friend's senses and reintroducing them. Allow yourself time to experience a lack of sight, sound or movement, and see where the experience takes you emotionally. Discuss this with your friend or partner afterwards and compare your experiences, you might also wish to write about what you "saw" when you were blindfolded, or "heard" when you could not hear the sounds of the outside world.

Exercise 7.6 is not for everyone. Some people can become very frightened at having their senses removed, and you need a strong basis of trust between you for it to work. If you feel uncomfortable with the notion of this exercise, do not do it. But if you do feel comfortable, the insight you get from it can be taken into your lovemaking – you might discover that it is very exciting to be blindfolded during sex, and that touch takes on a whole new dimension.

EXERCISE 7.6: HEIGHTENING THE SENSES

Time: One hour
Setting: Somewhere you feel safe
Music: None
Lighting: Natural
Props: Scarves or ties for blindfold and bondage, earplugs, cushion
Partner or friend: Required

Use this exercise to become aware of how important your senses are and what emotional and intellectual reactions you have to them being denied and then reintroduced. Only deprive each sense for five minutes at a time. This will seem much longer than it actually is. Start by; deciding which of you will be deprived first. That person sits comfortably on the floor, with their back against a wall, legs outstretched and cushions around them for support. Blindfold them, then sit in silence for five minutes. Do not be tempted to start talking to one another; it is important that the blindfolded partner experiences the darkness in silence, to feel the sensation of lack of sight and to note the pictures or colours that go through the mind or across the closed eyes. If your blindfolded partner starts to feel panicky, breathe with them, taking deep breaths in and out together. Fear is a normal reaction to being blindfolded and will soon diminish.

To cut out the sense of sound, put earplugs in your partner and monitor them for a further five minutes. Now wearing both blindfold and earplugs, your partner focuses on what they "hear" in their mind. This might be voices, music, or nothing at all.

Tie your partner's hands together, and their feet together. Make sure they are still sitting comfortably, with their back against a wall and check that they are all right. If they wish, you might touch them sensuously with scarves, feathers, silk, or even a soft whip. Allow them to take time to feel the sensations, which will be very different without the supplementary senses of sight and sound. After five minutes remove the blindfold, after a further five minutes remove the earplugs, and after a further five minutes remove the ties from the hands and feet.

Domination and submission for beginners

Fantasies about sexually dominating someone, or being sexually submissive to someone, are very common but are often misunderstood. The essence of domination and submission is eroticised power and eroticised powerlessness, which can only be explored if you have a trusting relationship with your partner. Erotic power is a sexual pivot around which many happy and healthy relationships revolve; its controversy comes from the power aspect. If you have ever firmly held your lover down while you were making love to them, or asked them to "take you" and pretended to struggle, or put yourself in a situation where you played at being overpowered before sex, then you have played with erotic power.

Erotic power-play enables you to yield to your desire for erotic domination or submission, within safe limits and for a short time. This can give you a very intense sexual experience and can add another dimension to your physical and emotional pleasure. To play at being the sexually dominant partner you need to develop and act out the traits usually associated with power: being direct and assertive; taking the initiative; showing confidence, leadership, and an ability to give directions and orders. These are the techniques of power. Clothing, lighting, sex toys and other props can visually reinforce this sense of power. The submissive partner has power too – the power to set limits to what you do and to stop the sexual play if it moves beyond boundaries they are comfortable with. This type of fantasy enables the enjoyment of power-play in an erotically stimulating but safe way. Although the experience is real, the situation is, obviously, not permanent.

TIPS: CREATING A DOMINATION/SUBMISSION FANTASY

Decide how far you wish to take the fantasy. Both of you need to discuss your limits clearly before you start, and solid agreements must be reached. Consider whether it is all right for your partner to restrain you, whether it is all right for you to be blindfolded, or have your hands or feet tied down.

Discuss all the possibilities of the domination and how you feel about them. Do not attempt to do anything potentially dangerous, such as tying your partner so they cannot move at all, gagging them, or putting anything over their entire face.

Keep your role-playing light and fun. Never play dominant and submissive fantasy games if you are drug- or alcohol- affected.

Use appropriate forms of address, such as Master or Mistress, Sir or Madam, or even Your Honour. Some suggestions for role-play are Cleopatra and her slave; femme fatale or homme fatale and the spurned lover; corporate executive and office boy/girl; handyman/woman and the bored housewife or househusband; officer and the new recruit.

Wear something to symbolise your role. Boots can symbolise dominance, a collar can symbolise submission, but if you do not feel comfortable with this, just being naked while the dominant partner is clothed can create a feeling of vulnerability and submission.
When you are in role you might decide to do a number of tasks – even the housework can take on a new erotic twist if you are doing it naked with a sexy dominatrix watching over you! You might wish to play sexually while in these roles, allowing them to help you make love in a different way. Or use these roles as a basis to re-enact a fantasy scenario.

On ending a dominant/submissive fantasy, remember to leave any notion of power and powerlessness in the fantasy realm, where it belongs.

INTERVIEW

SIBYL HOLLIDAY, SAFE-SEX EDUCATOR AND HYPNOTHERAPIST, CALIFORNIA. SHE IS THE CO-AUTHOR, WITH WILLIAM A. HENKIN, OF "CONSENSUAL SADOMASOCHISM: HOW TO TALK ABOUT IT AND HOW TO DO IT SAFELY."

I do a presentation. "It is never too late to have a happy childhood", on infantilism and how to explore your inner child in a very active manner. Some people find it erotic to be treated as a young person, some don't. For many people doing inner child work, it is important not to have any erotic

contact in that space. Those who do want erotic fantasies acted out in that space find a loving, responsible adult to act as a mother or father in a way which is physically, psychologically and emotionally safe – and obviously consensual.

I used to work as a professional dominant and I worked a lot with men who were interested in infantilism, the acting out of erotic fantasies while dressed as a baby or young child. Many of them had been abused as children, did not receive l enough attention in a large family or had had to grow up too fast. This often left them with erotic fantasies about being a child. Often they would want to be humiliated for being a baby; they would ask me to make fun of them or abuse them l for dressing in baby clothes. I refused to do this, as I do not degrade people in my work, and I also refused to punish them for wetting their diapers. After I explained this to my clients, I would discover that what they really wanted was to be loved and accepted, regardless of their sexual fantasies.

I do not do anything which is humiliating or degrading, no l matter what the person wants. If they want diapers changed, I do it in a loving manner. I do not punish them for normal bodily functions, I let them relax about something which they had thought of as shameful. I have taken lots of clients out individually to do childlike activities, such as going to the playground. I might see someone extensively, or on a one-off basis, depending on their needs.

I remember one client who was interested in being sexually submissive, and when I was dominating him I saw different looks flash across his face: a young, girlish face; an unhappy baby, and then an angry child. I talked to him about this and he did not know what I meant. However, as we began working together, I began speaking to each of these different looks as though I was speaking to different individuals. After I did that each of these people began to emerge. I do not mean that he had a multiple personality disorder, but that he had different inner children, who were different ages and all had different things to say.

One of his inner children I addressed was a little boy himself at four years old, who had given up on life and was hiding in an inner tomb from the anger of his strict father, for whom he could do nothing right. I held him for about forty minutes and gave him all the love I could, and then all the love I could call in from the universe for him. We did a guided visualisation where we imagined him coming out of the tomb and back to life. We spent a year and a half talking and dealing with all his many frightened inner children and got all of them to come out of the tomb. He was able to create a safe space for them and to let them know that there was a nurturing adult figure, whom he envisioned as a priest, who would always be there and would love them forever.

The most important part of sexual healing is to have compassion for yourself, to soften your heart and your belly and to understand that you are doing the very best you can do right now. You may need guidance from another but everything which happens to you happens for a reason, and you can be happy, no matter what your background. We all need to forgive ourselves – that does not mean condoning bad things, but accepting yourself, and you have to start there. If you have fantasies which are not consensual, recognise that we all have a shadow side – they are a clue or guidepost to something and you do not have to act on them. With the right facilitator your fantasies can show you what you need, and what you do not need, and what is missing in your life. When we were young and things were missing in our lives they started showing up in our erotic world.

Conclusion

I hope this book will give you the help and guidance you need on your erotic adventure. Sexuality is not just about gender and orientation, or the acts of sexual intercourse and masturbation. It is an energy which, when tapped into, can transform our sensuality and creativity. It manifests in many wondrous ways. Everyone's sexual journey looks different and there is not only one way to be "sexual". Sexuality will evolve and change as the seasons in nature.

I have tried to impart all the knowledge I have gained through my various life experiences - "as I receive pleasure, so the whole universe receives pleasure through me".

References and Further Resources

Books

1 YOU CAN GO HOME AGAIN
Ernest Borneman, *Childhood Phases of Maturity: Sexual Developmental Psychology*, Prometheus Books, New York, 1994

Jean Liedoff, *The Continuum Concept*, Arkana, USA, 1986

2 GONE WITH THE PAIN
Ken Dychtwald, *Bodymind*, Jeremy P. Tarcher/Putnam Books, New York, 1977

Julie Henderson, *The Lover Within*, Aquarian/Thorsons, London, 1993

Stanley Keleman, *Your Body Speaks its Mind*, Center Press, California, 1981

Ron Kurtz, *Body-Centred Psychotherapy: The Hakomi Method*, LifeRhythm, California, 1990

Harriet Goldhor Lerner, *The Dance of Anger*, Harper & Row, New York, 1985

Jack Lee Rosenderg, Marjorie L. Rand and Diane Asay, *Body, Self and Soul: Sustaining Integration*, Humanics Limited, Atlanta, Georgia, 1991

Alexander Lowen, *Bioenergetics: The Revolutionary Therapy*

that Uses the Language of the Body to Heal the Problems of the Mind, Penguin, Arkana, USA, 1994

Joy: The Surrender to the Body and to Life, Penguin, New York, 1995

3 KNOCK, KNOCK, KNOCKING ON PLEASURE'S DOOR
Riane Eisler, *Sacred Pleasure, Sex Myth and the Politics of the Body*, Doubleday, Sydney, 1996

Alexander Lowen, *Pleasure: A Creative Approach to Life*, Penguin, Arkana, USA, 1994

Gabrielle Roth, *Maps to Ecstasy: Teaching of an Urban Shaman*, Thorsons, London, 1995

4 IN THE HOME OF THE SENSES
Pamela Butler, *Talking to Yourself*, Harper, San Francisco, 1991

Alice D. Domar and Henry Dreher, *Healing Mind, Healthy Woman: Using the Mind-Body Connection to Manage Stress and Take Control of your Life*, Henry Holt, New York, 1996

John Grinder and Richard Bandler, *Trance-formations: Neuro-Linguistic Programming and the Structure of Hypnosis*, Real People Press, Utah, 1981

Leslie M. Lecron, *Self Hypnotism: The Techniques and its Use in Daily Living*, Prentice-Hall, New Jersey, 1988

Stephen Levine, *Guided Meditations, Explorations and Healing*, Doubleday, New York, 1991

5 MATES IN HEAVEN
Margo Anand, *The Art of Sexual Magic: How to Use Sexual Energy to Transform Your Life*, Piatkus, London, 1995

Mantak Chia and Douglas Abrams Arava, *The Multi-Orgasmic Man*, Thorsons, San Francisco, 1996

Rosie King, *Good Loving Great Sex: Finding Balance When Your Sex Drives Differ*, Random House, Sydney, 1997

Jennifer Louden, *The Couples Comfort Book*, Harper, San Francisco, 1994

Pat Love and Jo Robins, *Hot Monogamy*, Piatkus, London, 1994

6 ANSWERS TO THE MOST COMMONLY ASKED SEXUAL QUESTIONS
Anal Pleasure and Health, Yes Press, San Francisco, 1986

Joani Blank (editor), *First Person Sexual: Women and Men Write About Self-Pleasuring*, Down There Press, San Francisco, 1996

Tracey Cox, *Hot Sex: How to Do It*, Bantam, Sydney, 1998

Betty Dodson, *Sex for One*, Three Rivers Press, New York, 1996

Leslie Kenton, *Passage to Power: Natural Menopause Revolution*, Ebury Press, London, 1995

Kendra Sundquist, *Menopause: Make it Easy*, Osment, Sydney, 1992

Cathy Winks and Anne Semans, *The New Good Vibrations Guide to Sex*, Cleis Press, California, 1997

Bernard Zilbergeld, *Men and Sex*, HarperCollins, New York, 1993

7 SENSATIONAL SEX
Pat Califia, *Sensuous Magic: A Guide for Adventurous Couples*, Richard Kasak Books, 1993

Nancy Friday, *Forbidden Flowers*, Arrow, London, 1975
My Secret Garden, Quartet, London, 1976
Men in Love: Their Secret Fantasies, Arrow, London, 1980
Women on Top, Arrow, London, 1991

Trevor Jacques, *On The Safe Edge: A Manual for SM Play*, Whole SM Publishing Corporation, Ontario, 1993

Wendy Maltz and Suzie Boss, *The Garden of Desire*, Doubleday, 1997

Ruth Ostrow, *Burning Urges*, Pan Macmillan, Sydney, 1997
Hot and Sweaty, Pan Macmillan, Sydney, 1997

Carol Queen, *Exhibitionism for the Shy*, Down There Press, San Francisco, 1995

Videos

Unless otherwise specified, the videos listed below are all available in Australia through The Pleasure Spot, PO Box 213, Woollahra NSW 2025, email: pleaspot@ozemail.com.au, ph: 02 9361 0433, fax: 02 9331 6120

Betty Dodson, *Self Loving – Women's Masturbation Workshop*

Pride and Terrance Higgins Trust, *Well Sexy Women: A Lesbian Guide to Sexual Health*

Joseph Kramer, Eros Spirit, gay and lesbian videos and audiotapes; also director of the New School of Erotic Touch, a cyberschool offering, massage and masturbation instruction for men. Contact email: kramer@erospirit.org, web: www.erospirit.org and www.eroticmassage.com

Candida Royal, *Sexual Fantasy Videos Made by Women for Women*
The Secrets of Sacred Sex: A Guide to Intimacy and Loving

Annie Sprinkle, *Sluts and Goddesses*. Other Annie Sprinkle products can be bought from Good Vibrations, San Francisco, ph: 415 974 8990, fax: 415 974 8989, email: goodvibe@well.com. For further information, see Annie Sprinkle's website at www.heck.com

Andrew Stanway, *Lovers Guide 1,2,3*

Debra Sundhal, videos on female ejaculation. Available through Good Vibrations, San Francisco, USA, ph: 415 974 8990, fax: 415 974 8989, email:goodvibe@well.com

Interviews

Hilary Armstrong, Therapist and lecturer in critical psychology, University of Western Sydney, ph: 02 9953 1346, fax: 02 9904 0487, email: hilpete@ozemail.com.au

Fleur Bishop, Social worker and counsellor, Bush Sanctuary Healing and Counselling Centre, 33 Peter Close, Hornsby Heights NSW 2077, ph/fax: 02 9476 3997, email: sanctuary@ozemail.com.au

Anthony Harden, Body worker specialising in men's taoist techniques, Perth, Western Australia

C. Moore Hardy, Photographer, Starfish Studios, 37 Burnie Street, Clovelly NSW 2031, ph/fax: 02 9665 9678

Esme Holmes, Jungian analytical psychotherapist, group processing, meditation and spiritual healing, Coeur D'or, PO Box 303, Annandale NSW 2038, Australia, ph: 02 9810 7164

Sibyl Holliday, QSM, PO Box 880154, San Francisco CA 94188, USA

Dr Robert Maciver, Relationships and sexual counsellor, 21 Whistler Ave, Unley Park SA 5061, ph: 08 8272 5060, email: robertmc@netspace.net.au

Shelly Mars, Performance artist, New York, USA, ph: 212 633 6492

Kevin Olver, Psychologist and clinical hypnotherapist, 1-30 Rutland Gardens, Hove, East Essex BN35PB, UK

Ruth Ostrow, sex and relationships journalist, c/- News Limited, 2 Holt Street, Surry Hills NSW 2010

Tuppy Owens, sex writer, PO Box 4ZB, London W1A 4ZB, UK, fax: 171 493 4479

Elisabeth Shaw, Regional Manager and Clinical Consultant, Relationships Australia (NSW), ph: 02 9635 9311

Kendra Sundquist, Director of Education Services, Family Planning Association NSW, 328-336 Liverpool Road, Ashfield NSW 2131, ph: 02 9716 6099, fax: 02 9716 6164

Samsara Tanner, Teacher of personal development courses, PO Box 477, Byron Bay NSW 2481, ph: 02 6872 1000

Alan Tegg, Sexual abuse and trauma issues specialist, Leichhardt Psychotherapy Healing Centre, PO Box 815, Rozelle NSW 2039, ph: 02 9569 9296

Veronica Vera, Miss Vera's Finishing School for Men Who Want to be Women, PO Box 1331, Old Chelsea Station, New York City NY 10011, USA, ph: 212 242 6449, fax: 212 242 2273

Sexual products and courses

The Pleasure Spot (mail order sexual products and individual sessions) PO Box 213, Woollahra NSW 2025 ph: 02 9361 0433, fax: 02 9331 6120 email: pleaspot@ozemail.com.au

Bliss (sexual products) 1st floor, 241-245 Lonsdale Street Melbourne VIC 3000 ph: 03 9639 1522, fax: 03 9639 1544

Sh! (sexual products for women) 39 Coronet Street, London, N1 6HD, UK   ph: (020) 7613 5458, fax: (020) 7613 0020 web: http://www.sh-womenstore.com

Human Awareness Australia (love, intimacy and sexuality workshops) PO Box 616, Queanbeyan NSW 2620 ph: 1800 672 195, web: www.hai.org

Healthy Enterprises (individual sessions and courses) PO Box 235, Semaphore SA 5019 mobile: 041 223 5179, email: lstowell@senet.com.au

Beyond the Ordinary (Tantra courses and Goddess workshops) Contact: Diane McCann and Robert Mathews PO Box 1284, North Haven SA 5018 ph: 08 8248 1281, fax: 08 8248 1406

Awakening Woman (courses in sexuality) Contact: Brenda Sutherland PO Box 2148, Prahran VIC 3181 ph/fax: 03 9521 5073, mobile: 041 151 6185
Paradise Promotions (courses in sexuality) Contact: John Mulliss PO Box 7706, Gold Coast Mail Centre, Bundall QLD 4217 mobile: 041 115 6645, email: jacflash_onthenet.com.au

Brain Sex (courses in sexuality) Contact: Patricia and Donatus Michalka PO Box 335, Wembley WA 6014 ph: 08 9383 9799, fax: 08 9383 7034 email: michalka@starwon.com.au

Index